ADVANCE PRA[ISE]
A SEA BETWE[EN US]

I have always been drawn to true stories. There is simply nothing more compelling than real life. *A Sea between Us* is not only true, but it is an exciting, heart-wrenching, hopeful, and wonderfully told story that is as important as it is beautiful.

DR. MARTY MAKARY, *New York Times* bestselling author, surgeon, and professor at Johns Hopkins University

I'm excited about this book, and I can't wait to see how Yosely's story impacts people throughout the world. Ivey captured something really special in *A Sea between Us*.

TONY HALE, Emmy award-winning actor, writer

I've been waiting for more than twenty years for this book. That's not an endorsement exaggeration. In 1998, I got my first real job at an advertising agency in Birmingham, Alabama, and learned how to write from a guy named Billy Ivey. I'm thrilled this book is finally here, and when you read this wonderful story of human triumph, you'll be thrilled too.

JON ACUFF, *New York Times* bestselling author of *Soundtracks: The Surprising Solution to Overthinking*

Gripping. Billy Ivey captures the trauma of human tragedy and the inherent loyalty in true love. This is *the* American story. It sheds light on dreams that persevere in imposed darkness and helps keep hope in our sight.

TRACY FRIST, teacher, writer, farmer, preservationist, and conservationist

A SEA

THE TRUE STORY OF A MAN WHO RISKED

BETWEEN

EVERYTHING FOR FAMILY AND FREEDOM

US

YOSELY PEREIRA
AND BILLY IVEY

TYNDALE
MOMENTUM®

A Tyndale nonfiction imprint

Visit Tyndale online at tyndale.com.

Visit Tyndale Momentum online at tyndalemomentum.com.

Tyndale, Tyndale's quill logo, *Tyndale Momentum*, and the Tyndale Momentum logo are registered trademarks of Tyndale House Ministries. Tyndale Momentum is a nonfiction imprint of Tyndale House Publishers, Carol Stream, Illinois.

A Sea between Us: The True Story of a Man Who Risked Everything for Family and Freedom

Designed by Lindsey Bergsma

Edited by Bonne Steffen

The author is represented by the literary agency of Alive Literary Agency, www.aliveliterary.com.

Scripture quotations are taken from the Holy Bible, *New International Version*,® *NIV*.® Copyright © 1973, 1978, 1984, 2011 by Biblica, Inc.® Used by permission. All rights reserved worldwide.

For information about special discounts for bulk purchases, please contact Tyndale House Publishers at csresponse@tyndale.com, or call 1-855-277-9400.

Library of Congress Cataloging-in-Publication Data

A catalog record for this book is available from the Library of Congress.

ISBN 978-1-4964-4850-7 (HC)
ISBN 978-1-4964-4851-4 (SC)

Printed in the United States of America

28	27	26	25	24	23	22
7	6	5	4	3	2	1

This book is dedicated to our families and our many thousands of Cuban brothers and sisters—especially those who have lost their lives seeking freedom. To those who are still looking forward to a better life: No pierdas la esperanza.

YOSELY AND TAIRE PEREIRA

This book is dedicated to my family and my hermano. Thank you all for believing that I could tell this story.

BILLY IVEY

AUTHOR'S NOTE

YEARS AGO, my lifelong friends, Chet and Mary Virginia Frist, called me from Nashville. I could hear the excitement in their voices as they told me about a man they had recently met: a carpenter named Yosely.

I was intrigued. I didn't know any carpenters.

Yosely had spent a few weeks building and installing kitchen cabinets for the Frists, but it only took a few days for a friendship to be formed. "You need to know this man," they said. "You need to hear his story. Everyone needs to hear his story."

Over the next two months, I met with Yosely several times, and he shared fascinating details about his life, his family, his friends, and his eventual escape from communist Cuba.

I started taking notes when we talked and found myself falling in love with the tone of his voice as he shared his heart and expressed so many of his passions, heartaches, and joys.

After a weeklong trip to Cuba with Yosely to see the places and meet some of the people I had come to know through our conversations, I agreed with my friends in Nashville: Everyone needs to hear his story.

I asked Yosely if he would allow me to tell it, and he agreed wholeheartedly that the world needed to know.

I am not a historian or an expert on communism or US-Cuba relations. I am just a storyteller who has been given the gift of a great one to tell.

Yosely's journey is remarkable. It is exciting, adventurous, gut-wrenching, profoundly sad, and exceedingly joyful at times.

It is not, however, unique.

His is the story of an entire generation, an entire country of individuals, families, and friends sharing the same reality.

Yosely Pereira and I have spent countless hours discussing the details of his life. Like any one of us, he's had trouble remembering various specifics as well as the people he has met along the way. With the best intentions, I have recast certain moments in order to tell his story in an inspiring, educational, and compelling way. Although the events actually happened, many characters are composites of different real people in his life. Some of the names in this book have been changed to protect certain individuals who may or may not still be living in Cuba. Yosely has read several drafts of the manuscript and has confirmed that the story we tell together reflects as closely as possible the major milestones of his life.

This book is my attempt at communicating the harsh realities that this man, this family, and their home country have endured and sometimes, by the grace of God, overcome throughout several decades.

This is an important story.

I'm forever grateful that Yosely allowed me to tell it.

Billy Ivey
March 2022

Our hearts were always united—even
when we were apart. We had faith and
love and dreams we knew could come true.
The only thing that separated us was a sea
between home and hope. And how wonderful
that this great nightmare of ocean was the
same beautiful water that connected us
and allowed us to believe in a better life,
a better story. Once upon a time . . .

INTO THE BLACK

MY NAME IS YOSELY PEREIRA.

On February 7, 2002, I escaped Cuba.

Under the cover of darkness and with the determination of a runaway prisoner, I left my home. I left my family. And—quite simply—disappeared.

Why?

Because I had to.

For her.

For them.

This is our story.

* * *

There is an indefinable magic to my home country.

Valleys rich with farmland, ideal for growing sugarcane, corn, fruit trees, and bananas; fields low and wet enough to grow rice; and towering palms sprinkled throughout the landscape—a deep palette of greens dotted with flowering trees of oranges, yellows, reds, purples, and whites.

Cuba is a land of abundant forests leading to mountain ranges housing coffee and tobacco plantations, outlined by waterfalls, cascades, and crocodile-infested swamps. The Island's iridescent coasts are traced by bright white beaches or black coral—as mysterious as the waters that meet them.

The Island is a natural wonderland so especially breathtaking that even Christopher Columbus was astonished when he saw it for the first time in 1492, remarking that it was "the goodliest land that eye ever saw, the sweetest thing in the world."

So why would anyone ever want to leave?

I once heard Cuba described as the most ironic place on earth. I imagine the person who said that was referring to the beauty of the Island matched by its bewildered population— friendly, proud, and passionate; downtrodden, desperate, and lost.

But it hasn't always been that way.

My grandfather was the administrator of a sugarcane factory in the 1950s. He came to Cuba from A Coruña, Spain, when he was just a teenager. Cuba was once known the world over as a place of unmatched beauty and opportunity, so he set his sights on the tiny Island and set sail toward a brighter future for him and his family.

He worked hard, went to school in Havana, and was promoted up the ranks at the factory just before Fidel Castro came into power.

*   *   *

In 1959, when he arrived in Havana with his band of *revolucionarios*, Fidel Castro installed a provisional government.

For a time, the lower classes prospered, but this was only a ruse to buy time until he built up the armed forces and security services—including a powerful, politically tied police force. Then, everything changed.

Castro signed into law the First Agrarian Reform, setting a cap for landholdings and prohibiting foreigners from owning Cuban land. Suddenly, my grandfather—along with hundreds of thousands of Cubans—became displaced, having to learn new skills and embrace a much simpler way of life. Almost overnight, his aspirations changed from wealth and success to mere survival.

Before the *Revolución* was even a year old, the bourgeois element in Cuba's government were removed or forced to resign. Then one by one over the next several months, media outlets were silenced. And within a few years, all private property—down to even the smallest corner shops—was taken and solely owned by Fidel.

This calculated degradation of humanity left an indelible mark of bitterness on an entire generation, a sadness marked by hopelessness and melancholy.

Cuba became a prison.

But we were about to be free.

* * *

JANUARY 13, 2002

It had been just three weeks since I approached my lifelong friend, Enier, with my idea to leave the only home I had ever known. The notion was something we had whispered about since childhood and dreamed about as young men, drinking beers at night in the dark alleyways of our neighborhood. But this time was going to be different.

I had never thought about building a boat. I was a furniture maker; not a sailor. But something had to be done, and this was the only answer that made sense. As it turned out, Enier had already thought the idea through and echoed my excitement.

"You are the best carpenter I have ever known," he said. "How hard can it be? If you can build a table and chairs, surely you can build a boat! I can get the materials. You just have to build it." He had already saved more than enough money to purchase the wood we would need.

Enier worked at the gas station in town and would, from time to time, siphon extra fuel to sell on *el mercado negro*. The black market. The government controlled all fuel consumption at the time, so Enier was able to make pretty good money selling a gallon here and there.

"We will buy the wood—piece by piece—and store it in your shed. When you are ready, we'll move it, and you can get to work. You can do this, Yosely. You must."

But how can I?

How can I leave Taire?

She will never forgive me.

The children won't understand.

What if I am arrested, or killed?

What if it doesn't work?

What if saving myself puts my family in danger?

What if I can't save them?

* * *

Over the next few weeks, I cut, shaped, sanded, and pieced together a twelve-foot glorified rowboat in the darkness of night, just outside of town. Enier and I found a ravine at the edge of an orange orchard to hide our materials during the day. We would cover the pieces with palm branches, sugarcane husks from neighboring fields, and windswept trash from town. At night, we would go to the orchard, and I would work until daybreak.

Enier stood watch while we devised our escape through whispers.

There were many nights when my wife would startle awake and find I wasn't in bed. More often than not, her panic would turn to deep relief when she would find me curled up next to my son in the early morning before sunrise.

She only questioned me once about my absence during those few weeks. My eyes pooled with tears as I asked her to please trust me.

"You know I would never do anything to hurt you. I would never do anything that doesn't honor you. Everything is for you and for them."

But I couldn't do it alone.

"We need more people," Enier said. "The two of us will never be able to get to freedom alone. I know others, Yosely. People who can help us."

"Oh, yeah? Who? Who is crazy enough to get in a boat that we built in an orange grove and paddle to America? If you know these people, you need new friends, Enier, because they are crazy."

"Rafael, Alberto, Javier. They all want to leave. They are all ready."

"You told them? What's the matter with you!"

I was furious. I simply couldn't believe he had shared our secret. Three weeks of sneaky, sleepless, scary nights; three weeks of wondering *when*, not *if*, I would get caught creeping out of the house or we would be arrested for wandering the moonlit streets of our town. Now I knew. It was tonight. We were done for.

"Take it easy, Yosely." He tried to calm me down, but I was enraged and erupted out of the ravine and ran toward him, ready to tackle him to the ground.

"They are ready to leave, Yosely. They can help us get out of here!"

The three men Enier mentioned were all friends of ours and often joined us in the dark alleyways—to drink and dream.

"And what about Neo?" he asked. "That would make six of us. An even number."

"No. Not Neo," I said, now thinking of each of the men named.

"Why not? Neo would dog-paddle to America backward if you told him to," Enier said, almost pleading for affirmation.

"My wife is stronger than Neo," I snapped back, my eyes wide as the full moon above us.

"But he is loyal to you, Yosely. He will help us. We need him." Enier took a deep breath and waited for me to speak.

I climbed back into the ravine and started sanding the sides of the boat.

"Well?" I said, after a few minutes. "What are you waiting for? Go get our crew."

A new routine began with this unlikely band of brothers. Night after night, different men would join me at the boat to help sand and waterproof the sides. We were never all in the same place at the same time because we didn't want to create any suspicion, but I was there every night. After my family fell asleep, I would make the hour-long trek on foot to the orchard, never taking the same route, but always arriving in time to work for a few hours before slipping home.

The project took a lot less time than I had anticipated. Using only the light of the moon and a myriad of materials collected by my friends, I built our boat in just thirty-nine days.

When it was finally finished, I looked at the boat and started to cry. Slowly, everyone gathered behind me and put their hands on my shoulders.

Enier spoke for all of them. "Well done, Yosely. She's beautiful."

Then, the weight of our entire lives—our families' lives— fell on us all. We stood there for what seemed like an hour and silently thought of what might be.

"Tomorrow, then?" Javier finally grunted.

I shot a quick glance at their faces, and my sense of accomplishment suddenly turned to panic.

Tomorrow?

That's too soon.

How can we be ready tomorrow?

What about our families?

What about our supplies?

What if the boat isn't ready?

The others waited for me to take a deep breath and answer. I nodded my head and then, "Tomorrow," we all agreed.

I returned to my tiny home to find my family curled together in a half-lit room, asleep on my son's mattress on the floor. I stood in the doorway to his room and watched them sleeping, breathing, dreaming. Suddenly, Taire awoke, startled.

"*¿Qué te pasa, mi amor?*"

I wiped my eyes and smiled. "*Nada, mi corazón. Todo es perfecto.*" Nothing, my heart. Everything is perfect.

To tell Taire my plan would be opening her up to indefensible interrogation after I was gone. The *policia* would no doubt question where I had gone. The less she knew, the safer she and the children would be without me.

I turned out the light and climbed onto the mattress with them. Four of us, about to be three.

* * *

FEBRUARY 7, 2002

The next night, I met my friends in the orchard and hid near the embankment with the boat until we saw a truck's lights break the dark horizon.

Neo jumped up immediately and started waving to the driver. "Over here!" he screamed.

Alberto grabbed Neo by the collar and pulled him down. "Are you crazy! You idiot! What if that's not him? You could get us killed!"

But it *was* him.

Neo pushed Alberto away. "You can stay in this hole if you want. Me? I'm going to America."

The five of us each grabbed hold of a section of the boat and dragged it up the embankment. It was heavy. Very heavy. Even though it was only about twelve feet long, the weight surprised us all.

"What is this made of, Yosely?" Rafael asked, straining to keep from losing his grip. "Concrete?"

The driver of the truck was a local drunk we called Conejo, which means *rabbit*—he was always anxious, jittery, and in a hurry. This night was no different.

"Get in! Get in! Get in!" he whispered over and over.

I could smell the rum on his breath from ten feet away. "Have you been drinking, Conejo? Really?" I demanded.

"Don't judge me, *imbécil*," he shot back. "I'm risking everything here. And I don't even get to leave this hellhole."

He was right. At least we had the hope of escape to get us through. Conejo had to stay. However, he was going to make about three months' salary just for driving his truck 130 kilometers to the northern edge of the island. Perhaps he was entitled to a little celebration.

Rafael handed him a fistful of pesos, which Conejo quickly shoved down the front of his pants, then smiled. "Now, get in and shut up before I change my mind!"

We lifted the boat and pushed it into the back of the refrigerated milk truck. Enier got in the cab while the rest of us huddled on either side of the boat, securing it in place so the bumpy ride would not damage its hull, bow, or stern.

Conejo slammed shut the heavy, metal back doors of the

truck and secured them with a lock. We were in complete darkness, all of us afraid to speak or move.

As the truck rumbled down the path scarred with canyon-like divots and grooves created by rain and tires, the boat shifted furiously and loudly from side to side. We were already being abused by the journey and we'd only traveled fifty meters.

At the bottom of the hill, Conejo stopped, got out of the truck, and began yelling and hitting its sides. "Find a way to keep quiet back there or the deal is off! You sound like you're having a party. Shut up or get out!"

It was not lost on any of us that our driver was both correct and crazy. We needed to secure the boat better so it wouldn't shift and bang against the sides of the truck. But Conejo wasn't following his own demand, screaming at us to be quiet.

"Kind of defeats the purpose of sneaking away, doesn't it?" Rafael whispered. "He is going to get us captured before we even get to the road!"

I put my finger to my lips and shushed him, then lay down on the floor of the truck, wedged between the boat and the wall. The others followed my lead and lowered themselves to the floor.

The first hour of our trip was uneventful, but we were all freezing. The air seemed to thicken the faster we went—a mixture of diesel fumes and frost. The roads to Playa Nazabal were only partly paved, so the boat violently shifted throughout the entire journey. Our arms and backs and legs were tensed and cramping throughout the drive as we fought to secure our cargo. This was supposed to be the simple part of our trip to America, but we were finding out in real time that nothing was going to come easy.

I don't remember much about the truck ride other than the cold. I do remember thinking about my family:

How will they react when they wake up and discover I'm gone?

Will the children think I deserted them?

Will they think I've been arrested?

Will Taire be sad or angry?

What will they do without me?

Did I leave them enough money?

What will they eat tomorrow?

What have I done . . .

Finally, the trucked stopped. We heard three short, loud knocks on the back door. Time to go. When the doors opened and I heard the ocean, I felt paralyzed. A hot flood of adrenaline coursed through my arms and chest, and I was overcome with fear.

I was not afraid for me; I was afraid for them. All of them. My family. My friends. The only confidence I could muster was through Enier. He was going to be fine.

No matter what, Enier Santos was going to survive.

* * *

I can't remember a time in my life before Enier and I were best friends. He grew up just a few houses from mine near the center of Cumanayagua. We had almost everything in common. His father, like mine, was a carpenter, and we shared the turmoil of younger siblings.

I called him *hermanito*—little brother—both because he was always small for his age, but also because I really did view him that way. He was family.

Even as we grew into adulthood, Enier's stature remained like that of a prepubescent teenager. He hated when I referred to him as little, but he never denied it. How could he? But what he lacked in height and weight, he made up for with intelligence—and he was street-smart, too. No matter what the situation, Enier was always confident with a certain sort of *knowing*, like he'd been there before.

Even when we were children, Enier would conjure up impossibly intricate practical jokes or schemes to trick some-one out of a piece of chewing gum, a cigarette, or even a shoelace. Yes, a shoelace.

One afternoon after school, Enier and I stopped to swim in a narrow irrigation ditch just outside of town, some-thing we did most days before we headed home. The rib-bon of water ran beneath an overpass that connected the paved roads with dirt and gravel ones of a neighboring town not far from where we lived. After a refreshing swim, we hopped on our bikes to hurry home. It was nearing sunset and we had strict instructions from Enier's mother not to ride after dark.

Señora Santos was a kind, soft-spoken, gracious lady. She always had fresh fruit or sweet bread, which she happily handed out to her son's friends whenever we were in her home. Their family had no more money or food than anyone else in our city, but she always seemed to have snacks. She was as strict as she was pleasant, though, and perhaps the only person in the world Enier was afraid of.

As we pedaled, Enier was suddenly jerked from his seat and catapulted over the handlebars. He landed in a ditch, the bicycle tumbling behind him like a dog being dragged by a leash. His shoelace had gotten caught and wrapped around the crankset near the pedal and sent him flying. It was hard for me not to laugh.

But this was a disaster. Not only were we going to be late getting home, but Enier had just broken his brand-new shoelace! No doubt, his mother had to wash the laundry for several households just to pay for proper laces for her son's hand-me-down shoes.

I helped Enier to his feet and made sure he was okay, and then I started laughing.

"Shut up, Yosely." He started to cry. "Now, I am going to have to wash Señor Gordo's underwear!"

Let me explain.

Enier's mother would sometimes punish her son by making him help her wash the neighbor's clothes. We called the man who lived at the bottom of our street "Señor Gordo." He weighed more than four hundred pounds, and I could not even begin to imagine the horror of handling his undergarments.

Then, Enier saw a boy from our school named Leon walking toward us. Enier quickly turned to me and said, "Just stand here and be quiet, okay?"

"What do you mean? What are you going to do?" I asked.

"Trust me, *hermano*." Enier quickly turned and greeted Leon.

"*Hola, León. ¿Cómo estás?*"

"Shut up, Enier." Leon was as smug as he was ugly.

"Yosely," he continued, "you should teach your little friend how to ride a bicycle. He could get hurt out here."

Enier gave me a look as if to say, "Watch this."

"You're right, Leon. I'm not a very good rider," he said. "But Yosely is. He's the best rider in Cumanayagua *and* Cienfuegos. Even better than you, my friend."

Leon seemed puzzled. He was a few years older than we were and was known to be somewhat of a bully.

"You think Yosely is better than me?" he asked.

"I *know* he is," Enier said confidently. "And if I am right, you have to give me your shoelaces. If I am wrong, Yosely will give you his bicycle."

"What?" I shouted. "Hermanito! What are you talking about?"

"You heard me. You're the best cyclist in all of Cuba. Leon, I bet that Yosely can race you to the top of that hill and get back here before you even reach the top."

I glared at Enier and shook my head. "No."

"Trust me, Yosely. You can do this. You can beat him. And you owe me."

I *was* a very good cyclist. Our school had a cycling team, and I was the best in my grade. But Leon was older and stronger and a member of the senior team at school. He laughed at Enier as he considered the wager.

"Well? Do we have a bet?" Enier asked.

"Why do you want my shoelaces?" Leon asked, confused about this whole situation.

"*¡No te preocupes por eso!*" Don't worry about it. Enier smiled. "Are you scared to race Yosely?" He was really pushing it now.

"Of course not. Yes. We have a bet." Leon was fuming mad.

Enier moved slowly and stood in front of us to recount the agreement. "Your laces if Yosely wins. *¿Listos? En sus marcas, listos, ¡ya!*" Ready? On your mark, get set, go!

And we were off.

The top of the hill was approximately two kilometers away. I pedaled as fast as I could—each push forward stronger than the last. The wind was at our backs and I pulled ahead, pressing up the hill, never looking behind. At the top of the hill, I made a quick turn and then raced past Leon, who was struggling to stay upright on the incline. I never stopped pedaling, not once, and when I arrived back at the starting point, Enier screamed, "Yosely! You did it!"

Turning, I looked back up the hill. Leon was sitting on the side of the road. He had never reached the top.

As we climbed the hill, Enier couldn't stop laughing. His plan had worked! Leon was sheepishly unlacing his shoes.

"Good race, Leon," Enier said, fighting to hold back his amusement. "I told you he was good."

"How did you do that? How did you ride so fast?" Leon asked.

"I didn't have a choice," I said.

Leon handed Enier his shoestrings, and we made our way home, Enier laughing the entire way.

"You and me. We make a good team, Yosely."

He was right. And that was the basis of our friendship—Enier's foolhearted bravery and street smarts, and my ability to power us out of the trouble he created.

And that is precisely why I couldn't let him go with us to America.

* * *

"Yosely, hurry!" Enier whispered. "This is it. It's time, my brother."

I quickly pulled him to the side of the truck, where I grabbed him by his shoulders and crouched to look him in the eye.

"*Hermanito*. You can't go." I said, quietly, earnestly.

"Get out of here, Yosely. We don't have time for games," he said.

"Enier, look at me." I shook him slightly and said again, "You can't go."

"What's wrong, Yosely? Of course, I'm going. This is us—you and me. Let's go to America." His eyes were pleading for an answer. "What's wrong?"

I quieted and released my grip. "Enier, you are my best friend. You are my brother. I love you, and I need you to stay."

He could see that I was deadly serious and he pulled away slightly. With lips trembling and a look of betrayal on his face, he begged, "Yosely. We're a team."

"I know, Enier. We *are* a team. That's why I need for you to stay. You are the only person I trust to take care of my family. You are the only one who can keep them safe. The only one who can help with the police when they find out we've gone. Please. I can't just leave them alone. I need for you to protect them. You're the only one. I need you. *They* need you."

I finally had his attention. "You want me to take care of your family? Me?"

"You have to," I said. "You are the smartest, bravest man I know. And I know they will be safe with you."

Enier stumbled back as if I had just struck him with my fist.

"You want me to stay," he whispered again, as if trying to convince himself of what he'd just heard.

Just then, the other passengers pulled the boat from the truck and it slammed to the ground—the weight of it was too much for them to handle alone. Conejo sneered from the front of the truck. "Get out of here! Go to freedom, you idiots. Yosely! You owe me a beer next time I see you."

Enier looked deeply at me. He took a long, staggered breath, then turned and hugged Alberto, Rafael, Javier, and Neo.

"*Vayan con Dios*," he whispered.

The other men all looked at each other, unsure of what was happening. But then Enier took a short breath and put his hand on my shoulder.

"Please make it to America," he whispered. "Please don't forget me."

His words pierced my eardrums. "Forget you, *hermano*?" I began to cry. "Never. I could never forget you."

Enier turned from me and ran to the front of the truck and jumped in the passenger seat. Holding his arm outside the window, he slammed it on the side of the truck, and they were off.

The five of us were alone.

A million miles from home.

Just ninety miles from freedom.

*   *   *

The water was cool at Playa Nazabal, chilling our shaky legs and feet as we silently waded waist-deep, holding on to the boat and pushing past the first break in the waves. The night was completely dark, except for the white foam of the waves' crests. Dark clouds masked the moon, making this a perfect night to escape.

As we made our way to the rocks at the northern point of the harbor, Alberto, Javier, and Neo climbed into the boat while Rafael and I continued to push.

The water was getting deeper now, and the two of us struggled to keep our footing.

We had to move beyond the inlet landing before we could board; otherwise, the tide's force could easily slam us against the rocks, smashing the boat to pieces. Moving parallel to the shore and the rocks, we guided the boat to deeper water. Once on the other side of the crashing tide, we would be able to rest.

Rafael is taller than I am, so he positioned himself on the left side while I stayed on the right—closer to the shore, pushing as hard as I could against the rocks and waves. My legs ached and my lungs burned with each lunging step. Suddenly, as I brought my right knee forward, I struck a coral snag mid-thigh.

I sank immediately, letting out a scream that was mercifully muted by the water. As I writhed beneath the surface, Rafael lost his grip and the boat began pointing inland, shifting quickly toward the shore. He pulled me above water with his right arm, clutching the side of the boat with his left. I remember thinking, even then, that he had to be the strongest man I knew. I regained my footing, but I could hardly stand because of the excruciating pain.

"You okay?" Rafael whispered.

"I don't know."

The others instinctively grabbed the oars and began paddling, chaotically. Rafael and I stayed in the water, determined to find a better place to launch the boat into the straits.

There was not a satisfactory or safe harbor on the western side of the jetty, just an oblong nook we would have to maneuver in order to avoid being slingshot back into the rocks that seemed to be drawing us ever closer to failure.

For the next hour, Rafael pulled the boat to the calmer side of the rocks. I was no help at all—limping ahead like a three-legged dog trying to retrieve a stick thrown too far. The water was chin-high most of the way. The three others in the boat splashed the oars in and out of the water but never found a synchronized rhythm.

The closer we came to our stopping point, the quieter the winds and water became. The relentless crashing of waves turned to an almost eerie calm. The water was now over our heads, so we had to carefully pull the boat to safety without any real leverage, trying not to gouge the bottom or damage its sides.

Rafael collapsed on the jagged shore. The others surrounded him, offering him water. "No water!" I said, still whispering. "We'll need it later."

"It's only ninety miles, Yosely. We have plenty. He needs water," Alberto whispered.

"And we need him," Javier snapped.

They looked at me in disbelief, as if I were doing this to be cruel. But Rafael waved them off. "Yosely is right. We have a long way to go, and tomorrow will be very hot." He was lying flat on his back, panting and gasping for relief. Then he raised himself up on his elbow and pointed to the dark water. "It looks peaceful now, but soon we will be out there, alone with the sun. Put the water in the boat," he said.

The others reluctantly returned the water bottle to its position under the makeshift seat at the back of the boat, where we had secured the gasoline container, three milk jugs, and six cola bottles we had managed to collect and fill. Then they turned to me as if to ask, "What now?"

This had been a scheduled stop, but it was not our destination. I wanted to inspect the boat to ensure it hadn't taken on any water and make sure it could hold up under the weight of five passengers.

Our boat had never been in the water until that night. I didn't even know if it had been properly balanced. The mahogany and teak had never been exposed to rain, much less the sea's unrelenting waves thrusting against it with a force we could never have prepared for—not in a ditch in the middle of a field more than a hundred kilometers from the shore.

Our first true landmark sat due north, almost six kilometers away. It was an uninhabited island, and we knew we could get there before daybreak. This was all part of the plan. Enier and I had mapped our course very carefully from the shore at Nazabal to the island. If we could make it to that island, we could keep going—undetected because of the moonless night and by cover from a jutting range of nearby mountains—until after sunrise.

My leg was bleeding badly. The jagged, V-shaped gash from the coral was not particularly deep, but it was roughly the size of my fist. Alberto took off his shirt and tore it in half, creating a tourniquet to stop the bleeding. Even in the dark, I could see the bandage change from tan to black in the middle, my blood spreading like a slow sunrise. The salt water stung the cut with a dull burn, and my entire leg was throbbing, keeping tempo with my heartbeat.

After about ten minutes on the rocks, we pushed off—Alberto and Javier in front, Rafael in the middle, and Neo and I in back. We had two oars in the water—one in front, one in back, alternating left to right, left to right. Rafael began grunting, acting as a sort of coxswain pressing us toward the island.

I could feel blisters forming on my palms at the base of my fingers. We rowed furiously for close to an hour before the current shifted and began propelling us outward. We all looked around, surprised by the wind at our backs. For a moment, I thought we had been turned around in the struggle, afraid we might be heading inland again. But we made it.

We rowed to the island with time to spare before daybreak.

Relief set in, and we could finally speak without fear of being heard. "Get out! We need to rest," I said. "We need to breathe."

Truth be told, I needed to think. *What are we doing? Can I do this? What if the boat fails? What about my family?* The others all looked at me, wide-eyed and expectant, waiting for me to give the go-ahead.

"You built a good boat, Yosely," Alberto said, pulling me from my daze. "It's perfect. We can do this." I looked around at the others who all nodded as if to affirm their decision to go.

I put my hand on the boat and took a deep breath.

"*Vamanos.*"

I closed my eyes and my breathing slowed. The dizzying rush of adrenaline subsided and gave way to determination— all five of us stared silently northward, into the blackness.

2

NOT MY HOME

I LEARNED HOW to pray when I was very young—four or five years old. That's when I found out who god is. I knew that he was kind and loving, full of miracles, mercy, and grace. I knew what he looked like too.

He had a beard and deep, knowing eyes. He was strong and tall, with a high, domed forehead that made him look naturally imperial.

And I knew his name: *El Comandante. Máximo-lider. Señor Castro. Papa Fidel.*

I was given evidence of Castro's all-knowing power and generosity when I was in kindergarten. My teacher instructed us to close our eyes and place our heads on the tiny wooden desks in front of us. In unison, we were told to pray to God.

"Ask God to give you something sweet," she said.

Together, we all pleaded aloud: *Dear God, if you are a good and loving God, please give us candy.*

On the count of three, we all raised our heads, opened our eyes in expectation . . . and found nothing. No candy. Just our stone-faced teacher scanning her pupils as if to say, "I told you so."

23

"Now," she said, as she pointed to the six-foot oil painting above the blackboard, "I want you all to say another prayer. Close your eyes very tight and ask *El Presidente* for something sweet. One . . . two . . . three . . ."

Dear Papa Fidel, if you are good, if you love us and want the best for us, if you are truly wonderful, please show us. Please give us candy.

When we raised our heads this time, we found a single piece of peppermint candy resting on our desks. The instructor laughed with glee and clapped her hands. "See?" she squealed. "Fidel loves you! Fidel! Fidel! Fidel!"

My friends and I joined her in the chorus, dancing around the classroom, mouths full of miraculous sugar: "Fidel! Fidel! Fidel!"

* * *

My childhood home of Cumanayagua is a forgotten city, sprawled in the middle of a small valley near the Escambray Mountains. It's a beautiful place—typical terrain for the Caribbean—but somehow different from any other place in the world.

Small *chozas*, or shacks, fill the countryside—stacked cinder blocks, with palm branches loosely thatched to create roofs. Neighboring cities haven't changed since the turn of twentieth century, but there is something beautiful in the decay. Bright-eyed schoolchildren dressed in red, white, yellow, and blue; smiling townspeople waiting patiently in government lines for food and supplies to be distributed; and young and old people who know nothing of value, but for the communities they love.

I lived in a two-bedroom house with my parents, my grandparents, my two aunts, and my little sister, Yuny.

It was a tiny dwelling, but it was my home, and I was very proud of it. We all were. We didn't know anything different.

Everyone in our community shared the same misfortune: no one had more and very few had less.

*   *   *

My father was a small man—thin, but not gaunt. He was muscular, with well-defined shoulders, biceps, and forearms that rippled even beneath his loose-fitting shirts. He was incredibly strong—able to hoist bundles of mahogany, cypress, and pine planks on each shoulder and carry them from one end of town to the other without ever stopping to rest or reposition the load.

The large, visible veins on his arms and hands looked like a network of blue cables and lines connecting the tissue and bone. He had big hands, rough as sandpaper, disproportional to the rest of his body. They never seemed to stop growing. I feared his hands, even though he never struck me without good reason.

As a child, I never saw him smile. He was angry, plagued by the broken promises of hope. He wasn't mean or mean-spirited—just mad and sad and tired. He was never broken, though. The alcohol wouldn't allow it. And he never shied from letting his opinion of Castro be heard—especially after he had been drinking. Some nights he would have to be carried home from wherever he had been numbing his pain with *raicilla* or rum, when he could find it, but his voice was still loud and clear when he expressed his disdain for our prime minister.

At his very core, my father wanted a better life for his family. He wanted out of Cuba.

My earliest memories are marked by confusion. I couldn't understand why my father and grandfather despised such a great leader.

How could they not appreciate a man who fought for the rights of the underprivileged? A man who fought to end bigotry and poverty and to provide better health care and spread wealth to his people? At the very least, how could they not marvel at his ability to make candy magically appear on the desks of schoolchildren?

* * *

My parents took me and Yuny to a festival in Santa Clara when I was four or five years old. It was a street party on January 1 in observance of Liberation Day, a dual holiday commemorating the triumph of the Cuban Revolución, as well as the beginning of a new year.

My family usually avoided anything that celebrated Castro, but Liberation Day was different. It was a party that stretched across the entire country, a national excuse to get drunk and dance in the streets.

I remember being amazed at all the people in costumes and masks; there were thousands of balloons and flags and a small sputtering of fireworks at the end of the night. Yuny and I sat together and watched marionettes hop and bounce and skip and fly on a stage, maneuvered by a man dressed as a clown.

"You see that, Yosely?" my father said, pointing to the clown. "That is Fidel."

I looked at him blankly, but he continued.

"And that one, the wooden puppet on a string—that's you and me. It's all of us!" And then he swung his arm as if to capture the surrounding crowd in his story and erupted into laughter. He scooped up Yuny and began dancing in circles throughout the square.

My father was a known dissident to the locals and was occasionally abused by Castro supporters, both mentally and physically. I cannot count the number of times I watched while he sat in his tiny shop behind our house nursing mysterious cuts and bruises on his arms, neck, chest, and face.

When I was nine, I saw him cry for the first and last time.

I watched him through the candlelit window of his shop talking to himself—arguing with no one. He was like a madman, fist-fighting a ghost, switching from uncontrolled anger to laughter to tears.

He was drunk, and he was bleeding from above his left eye.

Earlier in the day, when my father was walking home from work at the mill where he loaded trucks with wood, he was ambushed and beaten by several men—people he knew—while members of the National Revolutionary Police aimed their rifles at the scrum, laughing and encouraging the men to teach my father a lesson.

*   *   *

Despite our circumstances, I was a very happy child. My early years were probably not that different from the innocence that most young people enjoy throughout the world: content and carefree. Full of fun and games. I loved my family. I loved my friends. And I loved my home.

A large part of my memory is wrapped in fondness. My life was normal. It was fine.

Our lack of money—or anything of real value, including clothing and shoes—made our parents resort to all kinds of ingenious ideas to make us not look completely destitute: flat bicycle tires were turned into shoes and belts; sugar or coffee sacks provided material for shirts and pants; and discarded bed sheets or fabric from worn couch cushions were fashioned into underwear.

From my young perspective, everything was as it should have been.

* * *

I spent most of my waking hours riding my bicycle, playing baseball, or trying to organize a soccer game in the park across from my school.

My friends and I would bind our socks and T-shirts with cardboard or soft plastic to form balls, and we would pretend to be our favorite *fútbol* players from the Leones del Caribe, or baseball heroes competing in our own World Series: the *Vaqueros* vs. the *Bandilitos*.

I was five years older than Yuny. By the time I was ten, I was very protective of her. More like a doting uncle or—dare I say—a father than a brother. In return, she looked up to me the way only younger siblings do. I was her hero. I could do no wrong.

She wanted to be just like me.

Our parents loved us very much and provided proper instruction and guidance, but they did so at arm's length. They never hugged us, consoled us, or kissed us good night, but Yuny and I were very close.

Sometimes, we would lie awake at night and I would tell her stories: made-up fairy tales about princesses and magical places where everyone was happy and the streets, trees, houses, and even the grass were made of sugar and frosting and colorful candies, free for everyone.

We would laugh and play, and Yuny would beg, "More, Yosely. Tell me more . . ." until angry "shhhhhs!" erupted from the other room.

Unlike my friends with younger siblings, who wanted nothing more than to show their dominance by keeping their brothers and sisters at bay, I enjoyed my Yuny's company.

Yuny learned how to play soccer, throw a baseball, ride a bike, and skip rocks into the river. She didn't experience the childhood most little girls have. There were no dolls in our house, no tea parties, no dress-up, makeup, or games of pretend.

As tough as she was, she was still a little girl, and I was proud to guide her, teach her, and keep her safe.

Yuny knew how much I enjoyed school when I was her age. She remembered with great detail how I would describe my days.

"Mathematics, reading, writing, and occasional experiments with food coloring or finger paints."

As Yuny walked across the street for her first day of

organized kindergarten, she turned and yelled, "Yosely! If Fidel gives me candy today, I will share it with you, okay?"

* * *

That afternoon, I was playing soccer in the park when I heard a large group of people screaming and chanting and arguing from the direction of my house.

My friends and I raced across the courtyard to find what looked like a thousand people—some I knew, others I'd never seen before—throwing eggs, rotten fruit, raw meat, and even rocks at my house.

The crowd was so dense, I was able to squeeze my way through and around to the back gate without being noticed. My father was on the front porch hurling expletives and throwing whatever he could find at the crowd. My mother was sobbing and begging for him to come inside.

"Please stop, Juan. Please come inside! They're going to kill you!" she screamed.

I raced through the back of the house to the kitchen pantry and grabbed a carton of eggs.

The front of our tiny house was now covered with fetid slime, but I wasn't going to go down without a fight. I was able to access the roof of the house by climbing a stack of crates near the back door. From there, I was able to shelter at the pitch of the roof, which became a perfect launchpad for heaving the eggs at the unsuspecting trespassers.

I threw the first egg and watched the yolk explode against a rioter's forehead. And another. Direct hit!

My aim was true as I flung another one, smashing it

against the back of a police officer. He whipped around and looked up. When our eyes met, I swear I saw him smile as several men stormed past our front gate and began attacking my father and grandfather.

There is no way to adequately describe the horror of seeing people you love being beaten. My vision blurred through tears, and I released a silent scream from the rooftop.

Please stop.

Please leave them alone.

Please go.

Please.

"This is your home, Juan Pereira!" the policia sneered.

"Fidel is your leader, Juan Pereira. Accept it, Juan! You will stop trying to leave your home, Juan Pereira! You will! Fidel is your leader!"

Over and over, the men kept kicking, hitting, and yelling at my father. Even in the moment, it resonated with me that they were calling him by name.

This was personal.

"Juan Pereira! Juan Pereira! Juan Pereira!"

Suddenly, the crowd parted as if pulled by a giant magnet; they pushed away from each other as aggressively as they had come together.

Three police officers were making their way from across the street. And then I heard an unforgettable sound. My sister's tiny voice—crying, screaming, pleading.

The lead officer was dragging Yuny by her hair while the other two tried to secure her flailing feet. She was fighting to get free, and they were laughing, dragging her, pushing her, spitting in her face, and using her hair to spread the saliva.

They were calling her a whore.

When they got to the house, they threw Yuny into the front yard. Immediately, my mother raced to pick her up and carry her inside. I sat frozen on the roof and watched the crowd disperse. My grandmother and aunts tended to my father and grandfather while I disappeared behind the A-frame and wept.

Fidel's followers did this?

Castro's people?

This is our savior?

What kind of leader allows a five-year-old child to be dragged from her school?

To be spat on?

To be called a whore and told not to come back until her family pledges allegiance to El Presidente?

Who is this man?

He is no god.

Perhaps my father is right. Maybe there is no god after all.

My life changed forever that day on the roof of my house. I knew, once and for all, that Castro's Cuba could never be my home.

* * *

FEBRUARY 8, 2002

The Atlantic Ocean is breathtaking at dawn. Sunlight glints across the water like a flame through antique glass. The horizon bends at the edges, calling into question the sanity of ancient poets, philosophers, and historians who claimed the earth was flat.

One look beyond those unending waters and it becomes dramatically clear: The earth is a perfect ball, floating weightlessly through the heavens.

Our first sunrise on the boat brought an unexpected flood of emotion. It was completely silent but for the lapping of uneven waters meeting the hull. No one uttered a sound. As the shadow of night lifted and light reflected on the water, I looked at my companions. *My friends.* They were all silently sobbing, tears spilling down their grimy cheeks, even the most stoic among them overcome with emotion.

I touched my face. I was weeping too. Perhaps it was exhaustion. Perhaps the bigness of where we found ourselves after a night of endless rowing was just too much to hold inside. Or maybe it was the collective realization that for the first time in our lives, we were not inextricably bound to Cuba.

We had been rowing nonstop for more than six hours since pushing off from the island. One of us would take a break every half hour while the other four rowed: one, two, three, four, pause. One, two, three, four, pause. Our hands were swollen and bleeding. Our backs ached, and muscle cramps in our legs were already threatening the journey.

But then came daylight, and we finally felt safe. Maybe for the first time in our lives. Completely drained of even the slightest bit of adrenaline, we allowed ourselves to absorb the weight of our emotions, and one by one, fell asleep.

After what seemed like only a few moments, I was startled awake by a loud banging and then a splash.

¡Estamos aquí! We're here! I thought.

I screamed even before opening my eyes, then sat up expectantly to catch sight of the Promised Land. But there was nothing. Only water and sky. The boat began jostling back and forth, waves reaching the top edges. Finally, the others woke to see me crouching above them, holding on to both sides of the craft.

Rubbing their swollen eyes, they all looked confused.

"*¿Qué esta pasando?*" What's going on? Neo asked, disappointed that he was no longer dreaming.

"We hit something. There must be debris in the water," I said. "Probably a log."

Leaning over the edge to look for the flotsam, I was met by an ominous shadow heading straight for us. A gray mass approaching like a rolling storm cloud beneath the surface.

Suddenly a fin broke the water.

Neo grabbed my arm and jerked me back to the center of the boat. As we fell backward onto the others, Javier screamed, "*¡Tiburón!*"

Shark. First, one. Then another. And another. We were surrounded. They charged toward the boat, changing direction just inches before collision and barely brushing its sides with each pass—just enough to let us know they were there.

"Yosely! What do we do?" Neo was panicking, his eyes wide and his voice rising into a steep scream.

This was not part of the plan. None of us had even considered sharks.

Rafael grabbed an oar and began to slap the water. Javier, Alberto, and I scrambled to join him. Fueled by fear, we garnered the impossible strength to make an incredible commotion. We screamed and slapped the water repeatedly, furiously, knowing that our lives depended on it.

The sharks darted back and forth, turning away and then swimming back to the boat—like lions pacing around their prey, forming a unified radius so they could strike.

Neo, my friend—my brother—huddled his tiny, shivering frame into the corner of the boat, pulling his knees to his chest as tightly as he could. His eyes were clenched tight. He looked as if he would explode at any second—veins bursting from his forehead, cheeks blood-red and puffed out from the breath he refused to give up. Even in that chaotic moment, I was struck by how feeble and frail he seemed, like a frightened child hiding in a dark room.

I had never seen him this way. Neo had always been the smallest among us, but far from weak. Far from scared—of anything.

He was orphaned before he'd even reached grade school.

The story goes that his father, a simple bean farmer in the western Pinar del Río province, became trapped beneath his tractor and was crushed to death while trying to help pull a government vehicle from a ditch near their home.

Upon hearing the news of his father's death a few hours later, Neo's mother opened the window of their fourth story apartment and leaned into the void.

Over the next few years, Neo moved between family members until he finally ran away for good and ended up near my hometown when he was fourteen years old. He was the smartest, most quick-witted, and most self-confident kid I had ever met.

He lived as a street kid, stealing fruit and bread and money wherever he could find it. The first time I remember seeing Neo was in the alleyway behind my grandmother's house. He was climbing a rain gutter, eyeing a pair of pants that waved like a signal flag from a line between the two windows above. He glanced down and smiled a big, toothy grin, placing his pointer finger to his lips.

I turned away instinctively, embarrassed that I had been caught watching him, but quickly turned back when I realized those were *my* pants.

"Hey!" I screamed, but he was already gone. Neo was quick as a cat and seemed to enjoy prowling about like one. I never saw him without a smile, and as we got older and began running in the same circles, I grew very fond of him. He was the type of person you think might electrocute you if you got too close. He radiated an energy I'd never seen before in anyone else.

Women loved Neo.

They thought he was funny and sweet. And he was. He was very popular in Cumanayagua—even the policia couldn't keep from smiling when he walked by. Growing up on the streets seemed to give him a false but seemingly unbreakable sense that he could do or get away with anything.

His laugh was infectious, he never lost at card games or dice, and he could dance the mambo, cha-cha, and bolero better than even the most famous *bailarines* in Cuba. Neo was one of a kind. Either the bravest or dumbest person I had ever met; I'm still not sure which. But given his background and the stray existence he'd lived through, I don't think anyone wanted or deserved to find freedom—a place to finally call home—more than he did.

"Neo, help us!" I yelled, trying to pull him from his trance, but he just sank deeper into the hull of the boat, rocking back and forth and finally exhaling, "No, no, no, no, no."

Before I could say anything, Alberto screamed and we saw a shark coming in fast on the opposite side of the boat from where I had been slapping the water. The predator's direct hit catapulted our tiny boat into the air for what seemed like twenty feet.

With a deafening thud, the boat met the water like a melon meets concrete. Everything flew into the water, including all five of us—helpless, vulnerable, and frightened beyond anything we'd ever known.

Alberto miraculously pulled his way back into the boat and threw an oar at a darting shark. The shark quickly changed course, allowing Javier and Rafael to climb to safety.

"Neo!" My scream pierced the chaos and seemed to echo over and over. I was still in the water, frantically diving under the surface, looking for our friend.

"*¿Dónde está Neo?*" I yelled to my friends who were reaching out their hands and screaming for me to get back in the boat. Suddenly, I spotted Neo floating about five meters from the boat and I swam as fast as I could. My legs were aching. My chest felt like it was on fire. My arms were hardly producing a splash as I swam.

He was floating faceup, eyes wide open, and there was a slight smile on his lips. As I approached him, he seemed to snap out of his trance and turned over to tread water.

Without saying a word, he swam past me to the boat, and the others pulled him from the water.

As we fell together onto the weathered floorboards, no one spoke. Neo crawled to the corner of the hull and began rocking back and forth again.

The rest of us looked at one another as if we'd witnessed a crime—unsure of what had just happened, unwilling to be the first to speak up.

The sharks were nowhere to be seen, but the sea was getting choppy and limiting our view. The waves resembled miles upon miles of rounded mountains, like silvery dunes stretching to the horizon.

About thirty meters to the starboard side, over the heads of Alberto and Javier, I could see the oar that Alberto had thrown at the shark bouncing up and down, moving quickly away from the boat. The other oar was behind us and seemed to be floating in the opposite direction. We began paddling the water with our hands, heading toward the closest oar while Neo sneaked impossibly closer to the sides of the boat, clutching his knees.

His whimpering began again. "No, no, no, no, no."

Once we grabbed the first oar, we all looked around for the second. It was gone. We didn't have time to think about what that meant, however, as the waves began to build, tossing our little vessel back and forth and forcing us to grab the sides of the boat for dear life.

Just then, Javier spotted the second oar and instinctively dove in after it. The waves continued to swell, larger and more powerful by the minute. Any control we thought we had was lost as a wall of water headed our way. Javier disappeared under the water for what seemed like several minutes, finally breaking the surface.

"*Mira lo que encontré,*" he said with a big smile on his face—and the oar in his hand. Look at what I found.

As the others pulled Javier back into the boat, I carefully crawled toward Neo. He was shaking his head back and forth, eyes still clenched tight. "Neo. Neo? Neo, listen to me."

I reached out my hand and gently touched his elbow. He shot to his feet as if he had gotten an electric shock. His eyes were open wide, and he backed away like a child cowering from a snarling dog. Suddenly, he stood up, pointed at me, and screamed, "*¡Es tu culpa! Tuya. Toda tuya.*" This is your fault! All your fault, Yosely.

Neo's eyes were different now. Like onyx stones, but without the shine. His lips quivered, and he began to shake—shivering like a wet animal. He was so completely in shock, I wondered if he could even see me.

Does he know where we are?

Where is he?

"Look at me, Neo! Look at me!" I reached out again trying to calm him, trying to keep him from falling over the side of the boat.

"Neo, calm down! Neo, sit! Sit down!"

And just like that, he seemed to come back. He quietly sat down, blinked, and then looked at me. His lips hardly parted as he said, "Yosely?"

"Neo, are you okay?" I whispered to my friend.

"There were sharks, Yosely. Sharks were hitting the boat." He sounded like a child recalling the details of a nightmare.

"It's okay, hermanito. They're gone now. We're okay. We're all okay. But you have to sit up. You need to hold on." I moved closer.

"I want to go home, Yosely. Please take me back home." As he turned his head to one side, a massive tear fell from his eye and landed hard on his shirt.

He slinked back down into the hull and covered his head, resting under the feet of Alberto and Javier. Their stony faces seemed to soften as they looked down on our friend. But I was rattled. Something was definitely wrong with Neo. It wasn't laziness. And it wasn't fear. It was something altogether different, as if he no longer occupied his own body. He just lay there, curled up, eyes open, but with nothing behind them.

Nothing but darkness.

3

COMMON HEARTBREAK

SOMETHING DREADFUL HAPPENS to the human heart after it breaks. It can be put back together but can never fully heal. The scars remain. They harden and begin to grow together, forming a calloused shield of protection—a thick wall that no one or nothing can penetrate.

It seemed my father's heart had been broken too many times.

Father was a gifted carpenter—an artist—who made beautiful furniture by hand. Everyone marveled at the things he would create. He was known throughout the region as the very best, and I learned a lot from him when I was young.

He would let me watch as he took a simple piece of wood and crafted it into a bed frame, table, or chair.

"Yosely, listen closely," he would say. "The guayacan tree will talk to you if you listen. It will tell you what it wants to become."

I believed him.

He would create works of art with just a few simple tools, as if the wood was willing itself to become something more beautiful.

He used to let me help sharpen his tools, scrape, and sand,

and I absorbed his great love of working with wood. He taught me a lot about the ethos of care and intentionality and taking great pride in the work. Like a sponge, I soaked up every trick of his trade, relishing not simply knowing the material, but knowing, understanding, and having a respect for where the wood came from.

Father taught me that wood is not like metals and plastics, whose properties are consistent throughout; wood is wholly inconsistent. It's stronger along the grain than across it. It expands and contracts more in one direction than another. Its color, weight, and grain pattern vary not only from species to species but from board to board.

My father believed that to work with wood—and to have it work for you—a person must first learn its complex nature: its grain, movement, and strength.

By the time I was sixteen, I had what amounted to a master's degree in carpentry, and I knew no greater satisfaction than seeing something come together and take shape—cut by cut, plank by plank.

"Do you see this, Yosely?" my father would say. "You helped make this. Do you know how important that is?"

I nodded yes, but I didn't actually understand what he meant. It was a rocking chair. Of course, I was proud of our work, but his question—the seriousness behind his eyes—reached deeper.

"Do you?" he asked again. "This tree. This piece of wood was intended for this purpose. It was created for you and for me. It grew in the forest for a hundred years for this purpose."

Tears formed in his eyes as he continued. "The wood from the tree has come full circle, Yosely. From being alive in the forest to being alive here and now. Perhaps an old man will find comfort in this chair. Or a young mother might soothe her child, back and forth, back and forth, on the curved bands you made. From the forest to us to wherever her purpose takes her for the next hundred years. That's what you did, Yosely."

*　*　*

The only thing my father loved more than carpentry was his family. I know that now. He was deeply devoted and incredibly loyal, but he was irreparably broken.

The scars of his heart ran deep.

The nightmare of reality shadowed his dream of creating a better life for his family, and rum became the anesthesia for his pain.

He hid it pretty well. Every morning, he would fill a plastic squeeze bottle with rum and sip from it throughout the day. He never appeared to be drunk, until he would pass out. More often than not, he was at home when he finally blacked out. Other times, we would wake up to find him asleep on the front porch or in the alley behind our house, where someone had kindly dropped him off or walked him home.

Drinking consumed my father, removing all that was left of his desire to fight against the darkness.

There is a certain machismo indelibly connected with being a man in Cuba. Part of my father's fall from grace came with the fact that he couldn't hold his liquor.

Real men are strong.

Real men work hard, drink hard, and fight hard.

Real men are always in control of their families, emotions, and future.

These, of course, are false realities in a police state—a country controlled by a master puppeteer—but my father fell deep into the disease and was unable to work. Unable to find the love he once had for our family. I remember the precise moment that I realized he would never return from despair.

I found him outside in the shed, sitting on a bucket, slumped over with his face smashed against the saw table, like a distorted and flat rubber mask. He had passed out holding a framing chisel that became embedded in the palm of his hand. He was bleeding and moaning, and he had soiled himself.

Yuny had followed me out to the shed without my knowing. When she saw the blood, she screamed and started crying uncontrollably, perhaps thinking our father had killed himself. She wasn't completely wrong, because as far as she was concerned, he died that day.

I don't think she ever spoke to him again.

*　*　*

When Yuny was a baby, Father used to call her his little butterfly, "*mi mariposita*," because she was a miracle. She had been born too early and wasn't expected to live, but my parents seemed to know there was something special inside Yuny that would transform her into something beautiful and strong.

And they were right.

She became a wonderful, healthy girl with a free, confident

spirit. She loved our father very much. I was always cautious about getting close to him, but not Yuny. She adored him and thought he could do no wrong. They had the same smile, the same eyes that sparkled when they laughed. The two of them shared a special bond that reached deeper than blood. They seemed connected somehow.

Maybe that is why it completely broke her heart to watch him drown himself every night in his shop.

*   *   *

My fellow passengers and I were burned and blistered beyond anything we'd ever felt. There was no hiding from the sun, no relief from the penetrating heat.

The twelve-foot-long boat was about five feet wide but very shallow, only three and a half feet deep. There were two boards, one in front, one in back, that we used as seat rests—enough room to get leverage to row. It was crowded and impossible to sit without touching another person in the boat—and particularly uncomfortable for Rafael.

His six-foot frame was bent over as he crouched in the back, alone on the board. Javier and Alberto sat in front of him, one on each of his feet. I sat with my back against their knees, and Neo sat quietly on the front board, entranced by the quiet lapping of the water on the hull.

Rafael is one of the largest men I have ever known. He looks like a bodybuilder, which does not exist in Cuba, but I had seen pictures of Americans with bulging muscles. Rafael's arms are as big around as my thighs, and his neck is the size of Neo's waist.

At home, Rafael spent most of his days as a laborer. He worked on farms, harvesting vegetables, tilling rows for crops, or clearing trash and other debris from public areas around government buildings.

He never officially worked for the government, but he was more than happy to haul off materials no one else was using. He actually had a lucrative black-market business, selling old car parts or discarded cinder blocks and rebar.

In fact, many of my tools were fashioned from trash that he had collected. He once helped me craft a planer from the front fender of a 1958 Lincoln, the same tool I used to build our boat.

I first met Rafael when we were in grade school. He was twice my size even then. I don't think anyone was ever scared of him, but we all steered clear of him on the playground.

He was never mean-spirited, and I never saw him angry; he was very quiet and kept to himself, which was even worse.

He spent a lot of time alone and often disappeared for days at a time. I found out later that he was working on those days. His father had started hiring out his son when he was ten or twelve years old, any time extra muscle was needed on job sites.

"Neo! Wake up," Rafael yelled from the back of the boat. "I can't get us to America by myself. You have to row!"

He was getting more and more frustrated with our stymied friend. It was hot. We were thirsty. Our hands ached. Our backs and legs were numb with pain. And Rafael was doing all the work.

"Neo, I swear to God," Rafael growled, "pick up that oar

and start rowing, or get out! I will throw you to the sharks, *idiota* . . ."

"Rafael! Stop!" I whipped around and met his eyes. "Enough," I said, turning back around. "Neo, trade with me. Let me row."

"Why do you treat him like a child, Yosely?" Rafael countered. "We had an agreement—we are all in this together— remember, *jefe*? Neo has done nothing but cry like a little boy since the sharks came. Look at his hands. They are not even blistered."

The rest of us were chafed to the point of bleeding. Alberto's hands were now wrapped in what was left of his shirt, and tears streamed down his face each time he pulled on the oar.

Back home in Cienfuegos, Alberto was a truck driver, delivering sugar, rice, and other dry goods from one end of the Island to the other. He was very smart and knew the roads in Cuba better than anyone, but he prided himself on never having to do manual labor—something for which he was now paying a high price at sea.

His hands were split on each crevice of his palms, like deep separations in the earth during a drought. He could hardly move his fingers without wincing in pain. Javier was blistered too. At the base of his right hand, large sacs of yellow fluid hung like bulbous grapes under the skin.

"*Está bien*, Rafael," I said. "It's okay. I don't mind rowing for a bit."

Without saying a word, Neo leaned slowly back and slid between my legs, allowing me to push up and take his place on the front board.

Left, left, right, right. Left, left, right, right.

Rafael and I made a good team. The waters passed under the boat at a speed we hadn't seen since the night before.

Left, left, right, right—faster and faster—as the swells beneath us grew.

4

I AM WITH YOU

EVER SINCE CASTRO took power, part of every young man's duty in Cuba has been to serve with the Cuban Revolutionary Armed Forces. After the age of sixteen, all able-bodied males are required to serve the government for three years.

This was Fidel's way of indoctrinating his citizens, thinking if they were forced to comply with his mission, they might even begin to believe it and fight for it.

All the men on my boat—except for Neo and me—had served in one way or another.

When my parents separated, I decided I was not going to join the army. I couldn't.

Who would provide for my family?

Who would take care of my mother and Yuny?

No one else had a trade or a skill, and my grandfather was too old. When it came time for me to report, I hid instead.

For three days, I stayed in the shadows of Cumanayagua, rarely going outside. Somehow, I thought that if no one could see me, the police would forget about the drunk carpenter's son.

* * *

I was arrested in the middle of the night. The knock at the door startled me awake, but it wasn't until I heard my mother's panicked pleading that I knew what was happening.

I rushed from my room to see three policia standing at the front door while a fourth held his arm to my mother's throat, pressing her to the wall. I ran to help her.

"*¡Suéltala!*" Let her go! I screamed. "She has done nothing wrong! Leave her alone!"

The three men rushed in and slammed me to the ground. I hit the side of my head on the stone floor and blacked out long enough for them to secure my hands behind my back with thin, nylon rope.

When I regained consciousness, I saw my mother crying in the corner of the room, covering her mouth with both hands. One of the officers dug his knee into my back between the shoulder blades, paralyzing and suffocating me on the floor. They quickly pulled me up, covered my head with a Cardenas Sugar sack, and threw me into the back of a government van.

I was told to sit with my hands between my legs and not to speak.

I couldn't see anything, but I knew exactly where we were going—to a military labor camp in Cienfuegos, about thirty kilometers from my home.

The ride was rough. My head ached and throbbed, and each time the van hit a bump, dipped, or turned, sharp pains would shoot down my neck and my back, all the way to my thighs. I became nauseated and called out that I was going to be sick. The guard sitting next to me removed the sack from my head and I vomited almost immediately.

"Are you done?" he asked, blankly.

I nodded, and he pulled the sack back over my head.

Cuban prisons and labor camps are overrun not just with criminals, but with simple men—fathers, brothers, and sons who get caught selling fruit or meat or even furniture on the black market.

Some were like my father—hardworking simpletons who either criticized the government or engaged in some kind of protest. If a prisoner complained or criticized anything, he was given extended solitary confinement, brutal beatings, and food and water restrictions, and he was denied medical care, or worse.

It was commonplace for inmates at this particular camp to harm themselves. Some people genuinely wanted to die, but others were hoping to gain release on grounds of mental instability.

The methods are often extreme: mutilating fingers, hands, and eyes; burning and cutting skin; swallowing sharp objects; and even injecting various liquids into veins.

I heard a story of an inmate at the camp who gouged out his eyes with a spoon. He had hoped to be released to the hospital, but he was taken back to the prison a few days later, blinded and in unbearable pain. He killed himself later that night by slamming his head into a brick wall over and over again. Prisoners who witnessed the suicide said his head had caved in like a rotten melon before he finally died.

Another man, serving a thirteen-year sentence for stealing an officer's bicycle tire, injected petrol into the veins on both of his hands. Prison doctors simply amputated his arms and returned him to his cell to live out the next nine and a half years.

When I first arrived at the camp, I was given a meal and told to eat everything on the tray because I would need my strength.

The plate was covered with rotten *patipanza*, a dish made from a cow's stomach and hooves. I lurched at the sight and smell and pushed the tray aside. Three prisoners scrambled and fought their way to me and devoured the meal in seconds. This labor camp was not like most prisons. There were no cells, no private rooms. All of the prisoners stayed in the same, large area—like a warehouse, but walled with cinder blocks ten to twelve feet high. Containers of humanity stacked one on top of the other.

Sewage leaked from one floor to the next, and the lower floors of the prison served as a paradise for rats, mice, and cockroaches the size of my hand. Most of the prisoners at the camp had been bitten many times.

"You'll get used to them," an older man encouraged. "They become like pets after a while."

Disease and infection were rampant throughout the prison. Unsanitary conditions led to debilitating diarrhea, vomiting, and sometimes death.

I suffered from chronic diarrhea for weeks before I finally figured out how to combat my upset stomach by chewing on dried stalks of sugarcane.

Like a cow with its cud, I was rarely without a ball of chewed-up grass in my cheek.

Prisoners were forced to work twelve- to sixteen-hour days, and they were punished severely if quotas were not met.

I was sentenced to serve just four months at the labor camp. My job was to harvest agave plants from sunrise to sunset in fields where temperatures reached more than one hundred degrees.

The agave is a large, thick, cactus-like plant with thorny spines. Nectar from the spines is used to make tequila, but it can also be used for medicines or additives in desserts.

The work was grueling and painful because we were ill-equipped and given few breaks for food or water.

On my first day, we worked almost eight hours in the field before we were given any water. Two prisoners collapsed or passed out earlier in the day and they were beaten in front of us—examples of what happens to those who could not follow orders.

A truck with large, plastic petroleum containers in its bed sat idling about thirty yards from where we were working. We were told that we had two minutes to get a drink and return. The containers were filled about halfway, and the guards took turns dipping buckets into them and pouring the contents into our open mouths.

The water burned as it went down my throat, and I had to spit it out. The canisters had clearly not been cleaned before being filled with water. I remember wondering if this is how I would die—a world away, yet so close to home, drinking gasoline.

Later that evening, on our way into the cell, I saw the inmate in front of me reach behind a small bush and slip something under his shirt.

Is it a weapon?

I suddenly became nervous and froze, watching the inmate look at another prisoner and exchange smiles. Just then, I received a sharp blow to my head, and a guard growled, "Keep moving, *imbécil!*"

The two suspicious men took advantage of my beating, using it for cover and moved closer to each other.

Maybe this is it.

Maybe this is how it all ends.

They're going to kill me.

I didn't sleep a single minute that night, fearing that I was going to be stabbed, or poisoned, or I don't know what.

* * *

Each morning, just as the sun's light made its way over the horizon, we were loudly awakened by guards banging on aluminum trash cans and screaming at the tops of their lungs. We were then forced to stand next to our pallets and ordered to bend down, touch our toes, and reach skyward three times.

Then we lined up and took turns washing our faces with water from a large bucket at the front corner of the room. The water was a disgusting dark brown and green, and smelled of mold and feces. Dead insects floated on top, and it felt thick, like oil, as I rubbed it on my cheeks and neck.

This was as close to bathing as I would get while imprisoned.

On the way to the agave fields, my neighbor once again reached behind the small bush outside our barracks, but this time he removed an item from his shirt and tucked it behind.

As we made our way to our positions in the line of agave spines, the man saw me staring at him. I quickly jerked my head away and pretended to be looking around the field.

"Amigo," he whispered. "You keep looking at me. Do you need something?"

"No," I said immediately, quickly shaking my head.

"You want to know what is in the bush?"

"No," I said again, shaking my head even harder.

The lead guard, a short, fat man with a bushy, wet mustache was coming toward us. He stopped directly in front of me and cocked his head, then met my eyes.

"You're new," he said, looking at my clean uniform, smiling. "Let me see your hands," he demanded.

He grabbed my wrists and turned my hands over to inspect both sides.

"No cuts. No blisters," he said. "Let's see what we can do about that." And then he pushed me forward into the field.

It was time to work.

That day was miserable. I was inexperienced, so I cut myself over and over again on the spines. When I wasn't working fast enough, I would receive a quick, painful blow to the back of the head or to my ribs. I thought the day would never end.

It took me several weeks to learn the process of harvesting:

Use a machete to shear off the thorns from all of the leaves. Cut from the bottom of the leaf all the way up to the tip. Cut the leaves surrounding the bulb until you get to the center of the plant. Do not try to pull it with your hands—that's like grabbing a hot iron from fire—instead, use your machete and cut it from the bottom.

As you peel leaves from the center you will find the corazón, the heart of the plant. Pull it toward you and set that aside. Dig at the base of the plant. Use your machete to remove the hard surface of the base.

Dig deep, and the guards will be happy.

Break the stem, and you will pay.

Every third day, we were all forced to clear fields covered in marabou. For lack of a more proper description, the marabou plant is a thorn bush that has run rampant throughout Cuba since the Revolución.

Without access to proper tools and equipment, farmers and landowners hadn't been able to eliminate the invasive weed that covered more than five million acres of agricultural land.

In prison, we called marabou *"la hierba diablo"*—devil weed—and were given machetes to attack it.

The thorns on the marabou bush can grow up to eight centimeters—three inches long. Sturdy as a nail and razor-sharp, the thorns can puncture skin even at the slightest touch.

Our shirts, pants, and gloves would all be covered in blood within the first hour of marabou detail.

At the end of a day in the fields, we all looked like defeated soldiers who had failed to advance a mission: battle-beaten, broken, and almost always on the verge of surrender.

* * *

It's a funny thing about exhaustion and fear. Either emotion by itself can make even the kindest person turn sour. Add in hunger, thirst, and unceasing sunburn, and it can turn deadly.

Literally.

Our boat was no longer full of excitement.

"All for one and one for all" had turned very quickly to "every man for himself." Something had to be done.

I wasn't sure how much longer we would be on the water, but we were not going to make it if we couldn't stay focused and become unified again.

"So, what are you going to do when we arrive in Miami?" Javier asked, hoping someone would take the bait.

But no one answered. Everyone just stared ahead as if in a trance.

Javier had been a teacher at an elite preparatory school in Havana before leaving his post to care for his ailing parents in Cumanayagua. He was the smartest person I had ever met. He had a degree in biology and psychology and had been published in the *International Journal of Cuban Health and Medicine*, examining the effects of iron deficiencies in rural populations.

I read the articles because I knew the author, but I never quite understood anything he wrote. It didn't matter though. I was just impressed that a kid from my neighborhood wore dress slacks and a tie to work every day.

When Javier's mother suffered a stroke, he abandoned his government-appointed position and illegally returned home. His mother died a few months later.

A SEA BETWEEN US

La policia and other officials didn't appreciate Javier's decision to place familial obligations over government duties, so they stripped him of all his earned credentials and made it nearly impossible for him to earn money.

That's when he connected with Rafael and the two began stealing and selling random building supplies on the black market.

A few minutes passed and then I broke the silence:

"I'm going to eat a big steak!" I said. "There's a lot of iron in steak, right, Javier?"

He looked at me a bit surprised, and perhaps honored that I knew his history—at least parts of it.

"And then I am going to drink an American beer. A Budweiser."

Javier smiled and grunted, "Cadillac."

"Cadillac?" I asked.

"I'm going to buy a Cadillac. A black one with red leather interior."

"A Cadillac. That sounds nice," I said, smiling.

"What about you, Alberto?"

"I'm going to find a blonde girlfriend with blue eyes!" he said, then laughed.

Everyone began to laugh, and the rowing started again. Everyone but Neo, who was now sitting at my feet grasping his knees to his chest.

"And she is going to teach me to surf," Alberto continued. "I've always wanted to learn how to surf."

I was relieved to have my friends back with me. *Maybe we are going to make it after all.*

Suddenly, Rafael screamed, "Look!" My back was turned to

him. Thinking we were about to be attacked by sharks again, I grabbed the seat. When I turned around, I saw Rafael pointing to a twelve-foot wave rushing toward us out of nowhere.

"Hold on!" he screamed, and we all braced for impact.

I guess we had been lost in our daydreams and didn't notice the oncoming storm, but the water turned from peaceful to chaotic in a matter of seconds.

The boat shot up in the air, and we all were thrown into the water like seeds cast out of a farmer's hand.

I hit the water, and everything went silent. I pushed myself above the waves to see the others frantically trying to turn the boat upright. Alberto was holding Neo up by his shirt. Neo was awake, but still expressionless—even as the waves came crashing one after another.

We all managed to maneuver through the water to one side of the boat and flip it over, using a breaking wave as a counterweight.

We climbed in as quickly as we could and held on for our lives. The waves were relentless. We couldn't yell or scream, because each time we opened our mouths, salt water would pour in, slapping our faces with the strength of fifty men.

The boat was almost completely full of water, but there was no sense in trying to bail it out. Thousands of gallons were being thrown at us every second. At this point, the boat was simply keeping us from being strewn away from one another.

I feared the bow was going to dip too far into the water and become submerged, and the entire vessel would shoot to the bottom of the ocean. But there was nothing we could do.

We simply held on for our lives.

*　*　*

At sunset, all of us made our way back to the barracks. The man in front of me repeated his actions from the day before. He pulled an object from behind the bush, but this time, he didn't put it in his shirt.

Instead, he handed it back to me.

"Can you read?"

I gave a slight nod.

"Hold on to this," he whispered. "It will protect you."

Then he hurried to the front of the line, never looking back.

I was shocked to find that the secret he had been hiding was a tiny leather book.

I immediately tucked the mysterious gift in the waistband of my jeans and covered it with the tail of my shirt. Being caught with contraband of any kind would result in a beating for sure—especially a Holy Bible.

I had heard stories of missionaries, secret priests, preachers, and religious dissenters being imprisoned, tortured, and even starved to death for proselytizing in Havana.

I wasn't interested in any of that. Besides, I never really understood the Bible anyway.

To me, it was just a book full of stories about people whose names I couldn't pronounce. And since it was illegal to own a Bible, I kept comfortably away from it my entire life.

The only god I ever knew took everything from me. He

took everything from my family. He had his people beaten, abused, and imprisoned for not following his rules.

I didn't want to know God. In fact, I hoped there wasn't one.

When I got to my cell, I quickly removed the Bible from my waistband and hid it inside the pillowcase on my bed, terrified and anticipating a pallet check.

Oftentimes, guards would demand that a random prisoner pick up his mattress, shake it furiously, and then repeat the process with his pillow, shoes, and clothes. To this day, I am convinced the guards were not looking for anything during pallet checks; they simply wanted to remind us that we had nothing—we *were* nothing. They also wanted to disrupt any sense of comfort or tidiness we might have established since the last check.

There would be no upheaval on this night. I lay there for hours thinking about the secret tucked in my pillow.

The next day, I found myself thinking about the Bible the entire time I was harvesting agave. I was excited to get back to the barracks and make sure it was safe.

It was.

And it stayed that way, untouched and undiscovered, for almost two months.

*　*　*

Some agave plants can grow between seven and twelve feet high. Their thorns, once removed from the stem, become like discarded shards of glass, baked by the sun.

In this particular camp, the government did not supply prisoners with gloves or appropriate shoes for the field. I was given house shoes—slippers with fabric on the soles—when I entered the camp, and that is what I wore in the fields.

I was a hard worker. I didn't talk to other prisoners while we were working. I didn't talk back to the guards. I simply did what I was told, hopeful that good behavior might buy me some grace from my captors.

Instead, I got very sick.

I developed an infection in my left foot when a thorn became lodged in the soft tissue where the heel met the arch. The infection brought a relentless fever that lasted days. I couldn't walk or stand, and my foot swelled to nearly twice its normal size. The guards told me they were going to cut off my foot if I didn't get better, and I hoped with every ounce of my being that they would. Instead, one of the guards lanced the side of my foot with a pocketknife to relieve the pressure and allow the blood and pus to escape.

I was in unbearable pain and was shown a brief mercy—I was given three full days off. It was during this time of solace that I remembered the Bible. Through fever spells wrought with bone-breaking chills, I removed the tiny book from its hiding place and opened to Isaiah 41:10:

Do not fear, for I am with you;
    do not be dismayed, for I am your God.
I will strengthen you and help you;
    I will uphold you with my righteous right hand.

I read the words again. And again.

"I am with you. . . . I will strengthen you and help you . . ."

I wept uncontrollably for what seemed like hours as those words echoed in my head. For the first time in my life, I saw the goodness of what a true God should be.

A protector and a provider.

A God who is with me and who will never leave.

I read that passage over and over and over again—committing it to memory—before shoving the Bible deep inside the pillowcase and trying to pray.

Please be real. Please give me strength. Please help me.

Three months, three weeks, and four days after I arrived, I was released from the labor camp—battered, bruised, and bent, but not broken.

I hobbled home with that tiny book still tucked into the waistband of my jeans—more determined than ever to get out of Cuba.

* * *

Lightning struck the sea, causing an explosion followed by the sound of a thousand shattered mirrors.

After the first strike, my ears were ringing so loudly that I couldn't even hear Rafael screaming. He was pointing over the stern, and then I saw what had made him so upset.

Our bag of food—oranges, bread, bananas, and apricots—was floating away from us. Then, another strike. This time the bolt struck just a few feet from us, and I lost consciousness as the eruption knocked me backward into Alberto and on top of Neo.

The storm raged for over an hour, and I was saved from drowning multiple times. My friends helped steady my limp body in the boat over and over again as the waves threatened to pull me into the water. Neo thought I was dead and crouched even lower into the boat. His panic probably saved his life that day as he lay flattened on the bottom.

When I opened my eyes again, the storm had passed. The sun was starting to break through the blackness above us, and I woke to find my friends using their cupped hands and arms to empty the hull.

"¡Buenos días!" Alberto said with a smile. "How did you sleep?"

My head was aching, but I forced a quick smile and asked if everyone was okay. "We're fine," Javier said quickly. "Your girlfriend over there still won't say a word or lift a finger."

He was pointing at Neo, who was still hunched over with clenched fists. "But, hey! That's what the rest of us are here for, right?"

"Oh, and I hope you're not hungry or thirsty."

Suddenly I remembered seeing our food drift away. We had nothing left to eat. And no water in the jug. This was bad. Very bad.

"No, I'm okay," I said, trying not to create more panic. "I'm saving my appetite for that steak in Miami."

*　*　*

When I was released from prison, home didn't seem like home anymore. I would see my father from time to time in the city. He either didn't recognize me or didn't care.

He was always intoxicated.

I used to feel sorry for him—he was so sad, so angry, so

sick, and so lost—but after being imprisoned, I became angry. I saw weakness. I saw a coward. I saw a shell of the man who had taught me about family and freedom, who had taught me about honor and truth, who had taught me a trade.

To watch him stumbling in the street, to see him passed out in the park, was like pouring salt in a wound that would never heal. I still cared about him, but he was not my father.

He was not even a man.

I started working from my father's shed, using his tools and making everything from broom handles to tables and chairs, bowls and utensils, and anything else people needed. My only goal was to provide for my family.

I was nineteen years old.

I worked whenever I could, sometimes through the night when the government allowed electricity to be used. When there was no power, I built furniture by hand—measuring with lengths of string, cutting with machetes or even sharpened stones.

I taught myself how to use century-old tools, hewing, hollowing, shaping, and shifting to create things even my father couldn't have done. I made good money as a carpenter, more than most of the people living in my town, and that caused jealousy and anger from neighbors and people I thought were my friends.

Police or inspectors from the government visited the shed almost every day. I wasn't doing anything illegal, but they shut me down for days at a time—sometimes longer, citing the noise from my tools was disturbing the peace.

I was very lonely. Most of my friends were either busy

working for the government, or they had moved to Havana or the town of Trinidad in search of a better life in the city.

I spent most of my days working, and my nights were spent alone—reading or thinking of ways I could get away.

But how can I leave?

Who will care for my mother, sister, grandparents, aunts, and cousins?

"I am with you"?

No. I was alone.

* * *

My entire life had fit within a ten-kilometer radius of Cumanayagua, with my childhood home at the center. Sure, I visited other places growing up, but they never seemed real to me. Just carbon copies of my city, my school, my house, my family.

When you are from such a small town—especially in a communist state like Cuba—you can begin to believe that the world is small. It's nearly impossible to see past your own circumstances and understand the vastness that awaits you but is just out of reach.

I knew there was more to life, but I could never have guessed there could be so much of it.

The ocean, for example.

From the shore, you can only see to the horizon. It's limited, landlocked, and stretches out only in front of you. The sky is the same way. It's a canopy of light we take for granted, except for a breathtaking sunset or threatening storm cloud.

Being in the middle of them both simultaneously is a different feeling altogether. The five of us struggled together for two days and were only able to focus on the stretch of water under each oar.

But now we floated in place, and I was captivated by our smallness in a never-ending, all-encompassing sea and sky.

Alberto and I sat silently, taking a moment to rest before waking up Rafael and Javier for their turn paddling.

"I am with you," I whispered to myself.

Alberto glanced up to see if I might be talking to him. I wasn't.

"I am with you," I said again. This time a little louder.

"Are you okay, Yosely?"

"Do you believe in God?"

"Which one?" Alberto said, laughing. "The only god I have ever known is Fidel. Do I believe in him? Yes. Unfortunately, he is very real."

"You know what I mean. The God from the Bible."

"I don't know," he replied honestly. "I haven't read it, and I don't know anything about Him. But if He can save us," he said with a smile, "I will believe anything you want, Yosely."

He paused thoughtfully. "Do you believe in Him?"

I looked up and met Alberto's eyes. "I used to. I used to think He was watching us, protecting us. But I don't know anymore."

I sat up, inched closer, and whispered, "I don't know if we are going to make it."

"Don't be silly."

"We're alone out here. Look around you. Nothing but ocean. We are alone."

I was almost pleading with Alberto to agree with me. Surely he could see how lost we were.

"Yosely, I didn't think we would make it through the first night," he said, looking up from his downward stare. "But we did. And we made it through the second night, too. Maybe God *was* watching us. Maybe He still is. And we will make it through tonight. And tomorrow. I believe *that*."

"We have no water. We can't make it through another day without water. And there is no wind!"

I started to become more and more agitated and anxiety began to set in.

"And our hands are ruined! Look at your hands! You can't even row!"

For the first time during our trip, I gave in to exhaustion and panic. Each man had had his turn at losing control over the past two and a half days, but I had been the constant up until that moment.

"We are nowhere, Alberto. And no one even cares."

Why would God save us?

How can He even see us out here?

"Yosely, we will make it—you will make it. We have to. Think of your family. Think of your promise to Enier. You just have to believe."

Enier.

I hadn't thought of Enier since we'd left him two days before. "I bet he hates me," I said. "Enier hates me, and he should hate me. He should be here."

"You were right in leaving him behind." Alberto inched closer. "He's your brother, Yosely. He loves you no matter what. God will watch over him too."

At that precise moment, a massive storm cloud covered

the sun and a dark calm covered us. I felt a raindrop. Then another.

"It's raining! Hurry! Get the pot," Alberto yelled, waking Rafael and Javier, who scrambled to secure the small metal pot that had somehow stayed in the boat during the storm, and began collecting rainwater.

I could hardly move.

Is this really happening?

"I was thirsty, and you gave me drink," I said, laughing and nodding to myself. Looking up, I shouted, "I am with you!"

I opened my mouth as the rain drenched my entire body, bringing instant relief to my face, my shoulders, my lips, and my tongue.

* * *

I went through a period of months where all I did was work—sunup till sundown—making and selling anything and everything I could in order to save money.

If someone needed a table, I built it. If someone wanted a gift for his girlfriend, I made it. If someone wanted the shirt off my back, I sold it.

Nothing was sacred to me; nothing but freedom, and I was prepared to do anything I needed to do to get it.

Unfortunately, freedom is not free—especially in Cuba.

On the contrary, it is very expensive.

I heard stories of men who paid up to twenty thousand US dollars for transport on airplanes. Others paid five thousand dollars just to be entered into a lottery where Mexican officials would offer only the chance of being selected as cargo on one of their trade trips. Still, others—especially young women—did unspeakable things to win the favor of embassy officials. The administrator of the government commissary in town offered to pay me three pesos and give me an extra loaf of bread if I would build him a rocking chair.

He was a very large man who worked for the government out of obligation, not allegiance. He was happy and kind, always smiling and making comments to passersby, trying to pull them from their despair, if only for a moment.

"*Te ves muy bien hoy,*" he might quip. You look very nice today. Or "*¡Es un bello día para estar vivo!*" It is a beautiful day to be alive!

He was a good man, simply doing whatever he could to keep from falling into the dark and to keep others out of Fidel's shadow as much as possible.

Every day he stood at the doorway of the commissary— sometimes for twelve or fourteen hours. He suffered from diabetes and had poor circulation in his legs, causing his ankles and feet to become swollen and purple. So the chair was not a luxury for him; it was a necessity.

I was finishing the chair runners on the front porch of my mother's house after yet another sleepless night when I saw someone out of the corner of my eye.

Love at first sight is considered a cliché, but the first person to claim it surely understood what the experience feels like. Your breath is ripped from your chest, leaving your lungs tingling with desire. You need to know and be known, to give everything, expecting nothing—without even knowing the other's name.

The very idea of love and the act of falling in love are at the same time foreign and intrinsic to every human being. And when you find it—or it finds you—love satisfies like water quenches a thirst. I saw her and I immediately felt safe—a combination of intrigue and calm, excitement and relief. I had been wandering, lost, aimless, and alone.

But that day, I discovered my North Star.

5

ESTRELLA NORTE

She was standing with another young woman on the front porch of the choza across the street, playfully chatting with the upstairs neighbor standing at his window—a seventy-five-year-old man, shirtless, toothless, and still drunk from the New Year's celebration the night before.

I whistled, then asked, "*¿Cómo te llamas?*" What's your name?

She was startled but aware enough to ask, "Are you whistling *for* me or *at* me?"

"*Hola*," I whispered and nudged a step closer to the porch.

"Answer the question," she said, expressionless, never taking her sparkling eyes from mine.

"What was the question?" I said with a smile.

"Why did you just whistle?" she demanded.

"I think you are very pretty," I said, smiling even broader.

She swallowed hard and quickly gathered herself. "That's not an answer. Do I look like a dog?"

"A dog? What do you mean? No," I stuttered, averting my eyes from her stare, as I took two steps back.

"Maybe a horse, then?" she continued. Her friend chuckled uncomfortably and reached for her to back up. But she walked down the stoop and into the small patch of grass where I stood with my hands in my pockets, kicking at the weeds like an embarrassed schoolboy.

"Why did you whistle?" she persisted with her questions.

"I just wanted to know your name," I said, looking back up at her and smiling. My heart was melting inside my chest.

"My name is Taire." She exhaled and turned quickly to rejoin her companion on the porch. "And this is Marena," she added, grabbing playfully at her friend's sleeve.

"Taire," I repeated thoughtfully, then backed away. The two of them erupted into childish laughter and ran inside.

New Year's Eve in Cuba is unlike any other holiday. It is the only day of the year when true harmony exists on the Island. Harmony . . . and alcohol. Some might say that harmony exists because of the alcohol, but I can't think of a better way to bring about patriotism in a place like this.

Supporters, dissenters; young, old; people in cities and throughout every ramshackle village in the country— everyone agrees on welcoming the new year with a party.

Each central plaza, large or small, fills up with beer-drenched men and women who dance and sing and drink and laugh, if only for one day and one night. They gather and watch fireworks rain down and make final, desperate toasts: "*¡A la salud, la riqueza, la prosperidad, y la sabiduría!*" To health, wealth, prosperity, and wisdom!

I also made this toast—this hopeless, empty prayer—the night before I met Taire.

She had been in Cumanayagua for three days to celebrate with her best friend, Marena. They had attended primary school together in Lomitas and dreamed of one day becoming teachers in the same school. They would move to Havana and live together in an apartment on the north side, near the Malecón seawall that stretches as far as the eye can see. Or maybe they'd find a place near Hotel Nacional where they could walk the Malecón into La Habana Vieja every day.

It was a long way from their home, but they knew they could get there together.

When Marena became pregnant a few months before she turned seventeen, her parents shamefully packed up and moved the family to Cumanayagua. She and Taire stayed in touch as much as possible over the next few years, but Marena's dream of becoming a teacher had been snuffed out by motherhood.

Cumanayagua was as close to the big city as Marena would ever get. Taire, on the other hand, was still committed to making a better life for herself. She had loved the simplicity of her childhood, but she'd been forever drawn to the bright lights, music, beautiful architecture, romance, and excitement of towns far away from home.

The Havana of her dreams was still the Havana of old— long before the effects of Fidel. Her view had been created by television and magazines that she would find in trash receptacles at the edge of town.

As far as Taire knew, the capital city was still a tropical playground where mafia-run restaurants, nightclubs, and pre-Revolución hotels sparkled and shined and pulsed with the energy and the beauty of Hollywood.

The opposite of Lomitas.

*   *   *

As a child Taire would wake more often than not to the tickle of a mouse or house rat nibbling the tips of her toes, nose, or ears. She grew up in the country, where vermin were so common, they were not even considered nuisances, so long as they were not destroying crops or what little food a family kept in the house.

Even though Taire was comfortable with mice scurrying underfoot, she never got used to the idea of them watching her sleep.

Taire's childhood home was made of palm trees, bundled together with dried strips of bark and string. The roof was a tapestry of dried mud, fronds, and plastic.

Her home was only about twelve kilometers outside of Cumanayagua, but Lomitas might as well have been on a different planet. Her family had no electricity. No running water. No markets or automobiles. The area wasn't even a village. Just a dirt road lined with tiny dwellings where shoeless children chased emaciated dogs, pigs, or chickens.

It was a section of territory that had seemingly been overlooked by the Revolución.

But it was a happy place. Her childhood was full of family, friends, and the joy that came from simply playing hide-and-seek or tag, or inventing games with their school neckerchiefs.

Lomitas means "hills" in English, and except for a few lowland farming areas, it was aptly named. Her family's land was never seized by the government because the rocky soil was considered unfit to farm. Still, her father was able to grow beautiful fruit trees, vegetables, and beans where most others would never have even tried.

Señor Hernandez is a large man, not very tall, but strong with broad shoulders, like a Brahman bull. In another place, in a different time, he could have been a movie star. He is very handsome, with deep, knowing, caring, and smiling eyes that shine like glass—cobalt blue surrounded by the whitest white.

Taire's father loved his trees and treated each branch like a member of his family. Taire and her younger sister would sometimes joke that they wished they were named Mango or Guava, because maybe then their father would love them as much as he loved his trees.

He would talk to the trees, which was probably incredibly entertaining. But he would also listen. That's what made some people think he had lost his mind.

Her father never picked a fruit or cut a limb unless the tree told him it was okay. Taire used to think he was playing with her, or just acting, when she would catch him in the fields whispering and even laughing with his trees—because everywhere else, he was silent as a stone.

Others were convinced that he had eaten too many anon seeds, which can be toxic and sometimes cause hallucinations. Regardless, Señor Hernandez's fruits were the envy of all who saw or tasted them.

Every morning, Señor Hernandez would wake before the roosters and begin tending his trees—clearing the ground around each trunk while running his hands along its bark as if trying to calm a spooked horse.

"There, there. You are a good tree—*muy fuerte*—a very strong and good tree. You are a good tree." Over and over, throughout the entire line, he would clear the ground at the base of each tree, touching and speaking to it before plucking its fruit or collecting his cuttings for propagation.

Early one afternoon Taire walked outside and up the hill behind their choza to find her father talking with la policia. The officer was pressing his finger into her father's chest and accusing him of selling his fruit. He was demanding money.

"You owe me," he growled.

"No, no. You don't understand," her father pleaded. "My fruit is not for sale. Please, take what you want. It's free."

The policia pushed Señor Hernandez backward and sent him tumbling down the hill. He rolled onto his shoulder and landed on his hands and knees, looking up at the officer, gasping and shying away like a dog. Taire started to run and make sure her father was okay, but he quickly ordered her to go back inside the house.

"Taire! No! Get away from me! You don't belong out here!"

He never raised his voice in anger, so his tone startled Taire and she ran inside, crying. Before turning to leave, la policia grunted at her father and urinated on a basket of mangoes Señor Hernandez had collected earlier in the day.

Taire watched as her father threw away the spoiled fruit with tears streaming down his face—not because he was hurt, but because his much-needed harvest could not be shared.

* * *

Late in the afternoon of New Year's Day, I saw Taire and Marena start up the dirt path that led from our barrio to the courtyard where people were still celebrating from the night before. I rushed to put on my shoes so I could follow them, but I could only find one. I stumbled through the house looking for its match, but it was nowhere to be seen. I couldn't risk losing Taire.

What if she never comes back? What if I never see her again? She doesn't even know my name!

I burst out my front door and leaped over the porch steps in one swooping motion, then limped barefoot up the rocky road as fast as my legs would take me. Centro Plaza was a myriad of joviality. Everyone was still dancing, embracing, sharing food, drinking, singing songs, and lighting firecrackers.

Later that afternoon, a parade of sorts would travel through Cumanayagua. Government representatives would move through the entire country in their Mercedes, waving to onlookers and handing out extra food and supply vouchers to the frenzied crowd. I hadn't planned on attending the festivities, but my heart took me there without regard for what would happen next.

And then I saw them. The two were so happy: laughing and smiling, skipping along together with locked arms like little girls on their way to school.

I made my way up and around the crowd and ran ahead without them seeing me. I found an empty spot on the corner of the street where I waited nonchalantly for them to walk past.

"Marena!" I called out, getting their attention. "And Taire, right?" I asked, pretending her name wasn't already burned into my soul.

The two girls stopped and smiled. "Nice feet," Taire said, nodding at my feet, trying to hold back laughter.

"Oh, yes. No shoes," I said, nervously. "This is a new style in the city. Do you like it?"

We all laughed at the absurdity of my bare feet as I brushed the dirt from my ankles.

"So, are you two here for the parade?" I was trying to think of anything to divert their attention as I moved a step closer.

"Why else would we be here?" Marena asked.

"I don't know," I said. "Maybe you were looking for me?"

The three of us spent the rest of the afternoon together, walking the streets and talking about the New Year celebration. As the sun began to set, I built up enough courage to ask Taire if I could see her again. She said yes, but only if I came to Lomitas.

The next morning, I gave my next-door neighbor, Guillermo, four eggs, a half pound of beans, a gallon jug of gasoline, and the promise of building a new kitchen table for his family in exchange for borrowing his motorcycle for the day.

I simply had to see Taire.

She was outside with her young nephew playing tag when I arrived at her family's home just after nine in the morning. I pulled up to the rough picket fence that lined her father's property and watched as she played like a schoolgirl with the grace of a ballet dancer. She took my breath away.

Laughing and trying to catch her breath, she looked up from their game and smiled.

Is it possible that she is even more beautiful than yesterday?

She waved, kissed the young boy on his forehead, tousled his shaggy hair, and then started walking toward me. I could hardly swallow. It seemed like she was moving in slow motion, and then she stopped, a curious expression on her face.

"*Nunca he montado en moto,*" she said. I have never ridden on a motorcycle.

She was nervous and still not fully convinced it was a good idea to go on a date with me. I took off my helmet and handed it to her. "Why don't you wear this? I don't want the wind to mess up your beautiful hair."

Laughing, she put on the helmet and carefully wrapped her arms around my waist, clutching her hands together tightly.

"Did you know that there are six hundred seventeen mango trees that separate you from me?" I said, as we rode off.

"That's a lot of mango trees," she said, unsure as to why I would know such a thing.

"Yes. That is a lot. Too many," I continued. "And it's a shame."

"Why?"

"Because that means I can no longer enjoy mangoes," I

said, shrugging. "I can't like anything that keeps me from you." I turned and winked at her, delighted that she had walked directly into my charm.

We hardly said another word for the next thirty minutes as we weaved along the potholed back roads from Lomitas through La Campana, toward Playa Rancho Luna. We only stopped once so that I could try to impress her with how much I knew about birds. I didn't actually know anything about birds, but I persisted.

"You see that bird fluttering near those berry bushes? That's a trogon. You might not know this, but it is Cuba's national bird."

"Really?" She feigned surprise at this fact that was common knowledge to anyone who had finished second grade. "Yes," I continued. "You see, its coloring—red, blue, and white—is the same as the Republic's flag."

It didn't occur to me that Taire had probably taught the lesson a hundred times to the children in her classroom.

"The trogon is usually found in forests and near streams," I went on, "but it likes to eat berries, and that's probably why it is near the road."

Taire's eyes widened as she slowly nodded. I was very proud of myself, and my own eyes shined a bit brighter as we rode off toward the beach.

*   *   *

We spent the entire day together, well into the night— following the stark countryside into the mountains, and then along the southern coast, where we stopped and ate orange slices and sweet bread I had stolen from my grandmother's cupboard.

When we talked, Taire looked at me. She saw me. She wanted to hear about my childhood and my family; she sat in awe of my love for cycling and carpentry. I told her about my sister and my friends. She listened intently as I talked about my father. I even told her about my time in the labor camp.

And she cried when I recited the verse from my secret Bible.

We sat and looked out at the ocean as the sun began to make its descent, and she reached for my hand. "Do you ever think about what's out there, Yosely?" She stared out beyond the shore. "Look at where the sky meets the sea. Isn't it beautiful? Where do you think it ends?"

I swallowed hard and let her hand fall from mine as I stood up and wiped my eyes. "America," I said. "And I think about it every day." Looking at her, I smiled. "It will be dark soon. I think I should take you home."

* * *

Stars appear larger in the mountains than they do in the valley. Pico San Juan, the highest peak in the Escambray mountain range, has an elevation of only about one kilometer above sea level, but riding along its ridge that night, with the forest closing in around us, Taire and I felt somehow closer to the constellations.

As we rode up the western ridge to the highest peak that led downward toward home, the motorcycle's engine popped, sputtered, and went silent as we came to a rolling stop.

"Yosely, what is it?" Taire forced a smile and turned her head slightly to the side and looked at me. "What happened to the motorcycle?"

"I don't know, the engine just quit. I'm going to kill Guillermo!" I huffed. We both got off the bike and I threw it to the ground.

I was both angry and embarrassed. I couldn't believe our perfect day was going to be ruined by an inept mechanic who was probably sitting on my front porch, eating a plateful of my eggs and beans, while Taire and I were stranded in the mountains, standing next to his piece of junk.

"Maybe it needs gasoline?" Taire offered softly, shrugging at the simplest reason she could bring herself to say out loud.

Oh, no. We're out of gas. How could I be so stupid?

"*Lo siento mucho. Lo siento tanto, tanto, Taire.*" I'm so sorry. I'm so, so sorry, Taire. That's all I could say. "*Lo siento.*"

Taire's eyes widened as if she'd just seen something terrifying, and then she began to laugh one of the most deeply genuine belly laughs I have ever heard. Out loud and unrestrained. She laughed so hard tears began streaming down her cheeks. I wanted to both kill her and kiss her.

But I started laughing too. What else could we do? I picked up the bike, swiped the kickstand with my left foot, and we both fell to the ground laughing hysterically.

6

FALLING IN LOVE

I DON'T KNOW the exact moment Taire fell in love with me, but I am fairly certain it was that night on the side of the mountain. I was forced to let down my guard and be myself for the first time since I'd met her. No more trying to impress her with my abilities or my knowledge of birds. I simply threw up my hands and we laughed together on the ground next to that stupid motorcycle.

After about ten minutes, we calmed down and wiped our eyes. "Now what?" I looked at her and we started laughing again.

We must have sat there and laughed and cried for an hour until both of our stomachs ached. We had to gather ourselves and come up with a plan.

"I need to find gasoline before it gets too late. Otherwise, we will be out here all night," I said. Truthfully, I didn't hate the idea of being stuck with her all night. I couldn't imagine a place I would rather be than with her in that moment and forever.

But we had to move. If the police passed and saw us stranded without papers, we could both go to jail.

"I remember a dirt road down the mountain, maybe a

kilometer back that way," I said. "There must be a choza or workshop or something at the end of it. Maybe there is gas that way."

She could tell that I was unsure of myself, but she nodded and agreed to stay with the motorcycle. I didn't want to leave her, but we simply could not leave the bike unattended for fear it would be stolen. Then I would be in real trouble. Guillermo would definitely press charges, and auto theft carries a minimum sentence of twenty years.

"I'll be okay. Just hurry back!" Taire said. And with that, I grabbed both sides of her face and gently kissed her. "I'll be right back," I said with a smile.

Did I just kiss her? Did she just kiss me back? The moment was so quick, so unexpected. So perfect.

The warmth of her lips lingered and filled me with confidence as I disappeared down the mountain. Nothing could stop us from being together . . . forever.

* * *

FEBRUARY 9, 2002

After two incredibly tiring days at sea, with no water and nothing to eat, our rowing was turning into little more than light splashing. We had lost all sense of direction. Neo was still silent, staring straight ahead. He hadn't picked up a paddle since we pushed off from the inlet outside of Nazabal.

Tempers were high and growing even higher, mostly directed at Neo, but it seemed that everyone was looking for a fight.

Alberto glared at Neo in disgust. "Look at me, *imbécil.*

It's time for you to row." Using his foot to nudge our friend from his trance, Alberto continued, "Did you hear me, Neo? Pick up an oar and row!"

Rage swelled within Alberto and he lunged at Neo like a big cat through tall grass. I rose up instinctively and took the full weight of Alberto's shoulder directly to my midsection. He sent me flying into the water, headfirst, and I was met with a deafening silence as I began to sink like a stone in the dark water. Rafael jumped on top of Alberto, pulled him off Neo, and pushed him into the water as well. Alberto splashed furiously and screamed at Rafael, who stood leaning over the boat with an oar, ready to strike.

Javier dove into the water and found me several feet below the surface. I felt a strange calm beneath the water, but he grabbed my arm and we began swimming upward. My lungs began aching and cramping for relief. When we reached the surface, we both gasped for air and reached up toward the boat's edge. Meanwhile, Rafael splashed the water with his oar, almost daring Alberto to come back in.

"You're not getting back in this boat unless you promise to behave!" Rafael sounded like a mother scolding her child as he whacked Alberto's hands from the side of the boat. "You have to promise. The sharks will be back soon. Promise me you will be nice."

The mention of sharks panicked Alberto and he started screaming, "Please! Please! Let me back in. I'm sorry. Please! I'll be good, I promise!" His pleas were high-pitched and fast, and he started to cry. "Please! Hurry! Please, Rafael!"

Javier and I were now back in the boat and began laughing at the ridiculous scene playing out in front of us. Our laughter caught Rafael's attention and snapped him out of his scolding. He stood straight up, proud of the lesson he had just taught our friend, and then Javier suddenly grabbed both sides of the boat and leaned it sharply to the right, throwing Rafael off balance and into the water next to Alberto. Javier and I were now laughing uncontrollably, pointing at our terrified friends who were convinced the sharks were circling just below their kicking feet.

Just then, Neo stood and extended an oar for our friends to grab. Our laughter stopped and the men in the water became calm. "Help me pull them in," Neo whispered to me and Javier.

Once our friends were safely resting in the boat, we sat in silence and stared at Neo who began rowing, slowly.

Never taking his eyes from Neo, Alberto grabbed the other oar and the two of them rowed together, well into the night.

*   *   *

The dirt road was farther down the mountain than I had remembered. I ran for close to an hour before I came upon the tiny, uninviting path that disappeared into the wilderness. I looked both ways—up and down the road—before carefully entering the jungle.

Gigantic ferns, most of which are taller than a person, and millions of palm trees dominate the mountains, forming an evergreen, humid forest full of flora and fauna that cannot be found in any other part of the Island. I walked along the path wondering if the sounds I was hearing were real or simply ghosts of nightmares.

When I was younger, I had night terrors—recurring dreams that I was lost in the dark and separated from my family. The dreams carried me to different places. Sometimes I was in the blacked-out halls of my school. Other nights would find me on the streets of my town or somewhere unfamiliar. Still other nights, I would be wandering in the jungle. No matter where my mind took me, I was always alone, and it was always dark.

Darkness is a common theme in Cuba. And I don't just mean the metaphorical kind brought on by oppression and depression and despair. In the daylight, the Island is a vibrant and vivid display of color and light—pastel-painted buildings stand out against a canvas of radiant blue sky; flowers and fruits and brightly colored clothing pop against the tan dirt roads; and the whites of teeth and eyes shine despite circumstances. In the light, there is hope.

But nighttime is different. There is an eerie quiet that arrives at the end of each day, as if the entire country is mourning the death of the sun.

For a few years during my childhood, I would begin dreading nighttime as soon as I woke up, my anxiety growing throughout the day. Yuny slept with me most nights and could calm my restlessness by singing me back to sleep. I wished she was with me at that moment in the jungle, aimlessly searching for gas among the trees.

After about ten minutes of walking deeper into the darkness, I came upon a tiny valley dotted with four or five shacks.

I couldn't be certain whether these makeshift dwellings were meant for animals or humans.

"*¿Hola?*" I bellowed to no one and inched closer. "*¡Hola! ¿Hay alguien en casa? ¿Hay alguien aquí?*" Hello! Is anyone home? Is anyone here?

There was no reply. I took a deep breath and crept toward the shacks, still unsure if I was alone. Immediately, I thought of Taire on the road. *She must be terrified. Maybe she thinks I left. Or I've been arrested.*

I knew I needed to hurry, so I quickly rummaged through each shack. The buildings were mostly empty, except for a few tools and some work clothes. Then I saw it—a small excavator parked inconspicuously behind the last building. This was a work site. A place the government was exploring for minerals—probably digging for quartz or limestone.

Next to the machine was a large metal gas can, probably ten-gallon size, and it was full. The can must have weighed sixty pounds. *There is no way I can carry this. And I definitely don't want to be caught with a government gas can.* But I had to get back to Taire. She was worth the risk.

I poured out all but two or three gallons of gas into the grass and then started running back toward the road. As I emerged from the darkness of the forest, the light from the moon and stars made the road as visible as if it were daylight. I stayed about five to ten feet inside the tree line in case any cars or trucks passed. I had to climb up and over felled trees and rocks and traverse large ditches and ravines the entire way, trying desperately not to spill the remaining fuel.

I was worried about Taire. What if she wasn't there when I returned? Did she wait? Had she been picked up by a passerby, policia, or worse? Each step became more deliberate than the last until finally, I saw the motorcycle ahead. I jumped out onto the main road and began sprinting toward the spot. I couldn't see Taire. *Oh, no! She's gone!* "Taire!" I shouted as I looked around frantically.

"Yosely?" Her tired voice whispered back from behind the motorcycle where she had fallen asleep. "How long have you been gone?"

Feeling a relief like I had never known, I exhaled and said, "Not long. What do you say we get out of here?"

Taire smiled and watched as I filled the tank and then heaved the can as far as I could down the winding road. She didn't even ask where I had gotten it. She just climbed up behind me for the ride home.

* * *

JANUARY 3, 1997

The next day, I headed to Lomitas to meet Taire's family. This time, I got to her house by hitchhiking on an oxcart for part of the way, but I grew impatient with the slow ramble of the beasts and ended up running to her door—smiling with each and every mango tree I passed.

I had never felt more alive. The feeling from the day before hadn't gone away. It clanged inside me like an iron dinner bell, and I was starving to see this most wonderful girl in the world, whom I had known only a few days. I was sweating and out of breath when I got to the gate of her house, but my excitement was met with her tears—not because of joy or excitement, but deep sadness.

Her uncle had died.

Taire ran to me and wrapped her arms around me. "Oh, Yosely," she sobbed, "you're here!" I hugged her as she told me what had happened. Her father's brother, Martin, had been helping in the fields earlier in the day when he collapsed and could not be revived. Martin had been like a grandfather to Taire. He was quite a bit older than her father and had served as the patriarch of the family for many years. Taire was very upset, but her sadness paled in comparison to her father's anguish.

As we made our way to the side of her house, her father was kneeling over the body of his brother, mourning his death in a way I had never seen. It was touching to see a grown man be so vulnerable and raw. In Cuba, no one cries. Not ever. Sadness is an emotion that has become anesthetized over the years. It's there, but numbed, like a tooth about to be pulled.

Taire's father was lying across his brother's chest, weeping and kissing the sides of his face. I couldn't imagine my own father crying like that. For a moment, I tried, but even in my dreams his eyes never wept.

Taire gently placed her hand on her father's shoulder, trying to console him, but he just kept rocking back and forth, feeling somehow responsible for what had happened.

My throat tightened, and I began to slowly back away. But then Taire's mother, a small, round woman with light brown skin and deep green eyes that smile when she talks, appeared in the doorway of the home and invited me to come inside. My heart was still racing, and I gladly drank the large cup of water she offered me amidst her tearful apologies about the situation outside.

"I'm sorry we are not able to give you a proper welcome, señor," she said. "Taire's uncle was a very special man. She loved him very much. She likes you very much."

I was becoming more and more uncomfortable with Taire's father wailing just outside the door and her mother trying her best to make me feel welcome.

But then her words connected as I took a sip of water.

"*¿Cómo?*" I coughed, spitting water back into the glass.

"I'm sorry," she said. "I didn't mean to embarrass you. But Taire thinks very highly of you, Yosely. I can tell she likes you very much."

My heart almost leaped out of my chest.

Just then, Taire came in and asked her mother to please go outside and sit with her husband. The authorities would arrive soon to remove the body, and the family would need to make plans for a funeral.

Her mother glanced at me and grinned with eyebrows raised, then gave a slight nod as if to offer her unsolicited approval. I believed then as I do now that Taire would have followed me anywhere, but she longed for that acceptance from her family—as if giving her permission to strive for more than that tiny, rocky farm. As happy and content as she had always been on the farm with her family, simply having me there gave her a hope in something bigger, different, and better.

We just didn't know what that would be.

We watched, numb and emotionless, as her parents grieved in the yard. They were crying from great sorrow, but also fear. Taire's uncle had been a pillar of strength in her life. He was smart and confident and strong. He took care of the family, including her father, who was soft and kind and "trusted too much," according to Martin.

"Your father exchanges money for smiles," he once told Taire, frustrated by her father's willingness to simply share his crops with anyone or everyone who needed or simply wanted the fruit.

Her father was like an artist, motivated not by money, but by the process of helping bring something beautiful to life. And it was not the fruit's taste or even its nutritional value that sustained him. It was his art.

"Your neighbors' smiles do not put food on your table, Taire," Martin would often tell her. "You need to be strong. You must never allow yourself to be taken advantage of like he does." Uncle Martin taught her the true value of family and taking care of her own.

Before the Revolución ultimately stripped him of his belongings, Martin ran a *mercado* in Ciego de Ávila, a city almost two hundred kilometers southeast of Cumanayagua. He was widely known as a shrewd businessman and was called to Havana to help with agriculture and trade when he was just twenty-four years old. Martin declined and instead decided to move home to Lomitas to help his family. And that is precisely what he did, for more than forty years.

Taire would miss him terribly. The thought of never seeing her uncle again filled her with a sadness that ached in her throat. But now, she had me. Maybe I could fill the empty space in her heart. I was certainly going to try.

Taire and I sat in her small home for several hours as friends and other family members came in and out to offer condolences and pay their respects to Taire's father.

"I'm so glad you are here," Taire said as she grabbed my hand and smiled. Her eyes were red and swollen from crying, but I could still see the truth behind them, and I smiled back.

The sun was starting to set in the distance. A deep haze filled the valley, warning me it was time to go home. The neglected roads between our houses were very dangerous after dark. Nighttime seemed to give the policia less patience for people in the streets and more authority to take them away. Unless you were in the city, or attending to government business, it was assumed you were up to no good.

As I stood to leave, Taire's grip tightened around my fingers. "Will you please come and be with me at the funeral two days from now?"

"I will go anywhere with you," I said, and a lump started to form in my throat at the thought of leaving her. "I'll be there." I kissed her hands and turned to go.

"My father wants to see you before you leave," she said. "He's got something for you."

I slowly walked toward the gate where her father waited with a plastic bag. He forced a smile and said, "Thank you for being with my family today. I am looking forward to getting to know you, Señor Yosely." With that, he handed me a bag of fresh mangoes, lemons, limes, guanabanas, and a pineapple. "For your walk home. For your family."

I took the bag and nodded cautiously. "This is not necessary," I said, unsure about how to react.

"Nonsense," he shot back. "Besides, Taire likes you. And if my daughter likes you, then I like you. We'll see you at the funeral?" he asked rhetorically, and then guided me through the gate.

As I turned and thanked him, I saw Taire standing in the doorway and smiling, then she disappeared inside.

* * *

JANUARY 6, 1997

The next thirty-six hours were the longest of my life. I felt as if a piece of me was missing. I needed to see Taire.

I spent hours trying to hunt down appropriate clothes to wear to the funeral. The extent of my wardrobe was three shirts—one T-shirt and two short-sleeved shirts with buttons, one of which had a largish hole near the armpit; two pair of jeans, both stained and worn through at the cuffs; a pair of plastic flip-flops; and an old pair of brown leather shoes that I wore when I worked in the shed. I also had a pair of brown cargo shorts, but even Enier, who wore shorts every day of his life, knew better than to wear them to a funeral.

I had to find proper attire fast. Javier graciously lent me his black trousers, but since he is about six inches shorter than I am, the pants legs hung pitifully above my ankles, exposing the white socks that shouted at my dirty, brown shoes.

As I was leaving home to make the trek to Taire, my mother met me with an egg in her hand. "We need to shine your shoes," she said. "You do not want to embarrass your new girlfriend to death at a funeral. That would be very sad," she said, with a smile.

She told me to sit down and remove my shoes. Then, she broke the egg into a small bowl, removed the yolk, and with a small yellow sponge, began rubbing the whites of the egg into the leather. When she had finished, the shoes shined like they were brand-new.

I made my way through the streets of my town, and several people commented that I looked very nice. Some of my friends—stationed on their porches, drinking beer—whooped, hollered, and whistled when I passed, making kissing sounds and poking fun at my shiny shoes and slicked-back hair. "Look at Yosely!" one of them called out. "He looks like he is getting married today!"

I felt ten feet tall, walking boldly to meet the love of my life. I held my head high and picked up my pace, trying not to run. I could hardly wait to see Taire.

I only stopped once, when a young boy kicked a soccer ball into the street and I veered to retrieve it for him. As I leaned down to pick up the ball, a small dog ran over, tail wagging and panting as if I were his long-lost owner. I petted the pup for a brief moment and then kept walking. For the next five or ten minutes, the dog followed just a few inches behind me, wagging his tail happily.

"Go home!" I said, scratching its head and pointing behind. It started sniffing and licking the tops of my shoes and then it hit me: the egg! This dog was starving and smelled food! "No! No! Go home," I yelled and pointed for him to go. But he continued wagging his tail and weaving between my legs. In a matter of minutes, a second and then a third dog began following me. All three of them were scampering so close to my feet I could hardly take a step without tripping over one of them.

I was getting closer to Taire's house, so I started to run. Only fifty meters to go. The dogs were running beside me now, growling and snapping at my heels. Thirty meters. Twenty meters. I was running as fast as I could, and the dogs were getting angrier and more aggressive with each step.

Ten meters to go, and I could see Taire in the distance. I started screaming, "*¡Cierra la puerta! ¡Cierra la puerta!*" Close the gate! Close the gate!

I reached the short fence in front of Taire's house and dove headlong into her front yard. One of the dogs jumped after me and circled me, growling, until Taire shooed it away with a broom. Exhausted and panting and trying to catch my breath, I looked up to see Taire standing over me, holding the broom and laughing hysterically. I started laughing with her and rolled over on my side to sit up. That's when I noticed my right shoe was missing. I looked around frantically and then realized why Taire was laughing so hard. The pup I had been begging to go home for the past forty-five minutes was finally obeying, but now he had my shoe clenched between his teeth—tail still wagging.

I sat with Taire and held her hand throughout the funeral. Every time she felt the urge to cry, she would look down and see my shoeless foot, toes wiggling nervously, and begin to laugh.

I was so embarrassed, but something about my vulnerability gave her peace. It was that day that I knew—shoes or no shoes—I never wanted to be without her next to me, holding my hand.

Every day with Taire was another reason to smile. I worked hard during the day, making tables and chairs, cabinets and doors, and anything else someone would either pay me to do or trade something for as payment. At night, though, I made my way to Lomitas to visit with Taire or help her father with his trees.

A few months later, we were lying in a field behind her home, looking at the stars and talking about nothing in particular, when I raised up on my left elbow and removed a small piece of paper from my pocket.

"I wrote something for you," I said.

"You wrote something?" she asked curiously.

And then I began to read:

Mi corazón me pesa, mi amor,
pero no por dolor.
Pesa como las hojas
después de una refrescante lluvia de verano.

Me traes esperanza de que la vida está cerca,
incluso cuando todo parece perdido.
Me has mostrado amor que nunca morirá,
y lo protegeré a toda costa.

Hay un lugar para ti y para mí
donde veremos algún día
la belleza de la vida juntos,
por toda la eternidad.

Ahora sé lo que significa sentir
el peso de la vida de otra persona.
Entonces, déjame llevarte, mi amor,
como tu esposo y tú, mi esposa.

My heart is heavy now, my love,
but not because of pain.
It's heavy like the leaves
after a refreshing summer's rain.

You bring me hope that life is near,
even when everything else seems lost.
You've shown me love that will never die,
and I will protect it at any cost.

There is a place for you and me
where one day we will see
the beauty of life together,
for all eternity.

I know now what it means to feel
the weight of someone else's life.
So, let me carry you, my love,
as your husband and you, my wife.

When I finished, I immediately felt like I was able to breathe deeply for the first time, and Taire began to cry. Then, with my voice trembling, I asked her to marry me.

I don't even remember if she answered the question. I just remember that she kissed me and hugged me as hard as she could, and she promised to never let me go.

A few weeks later, we made our way to La Perla del Sur. This is an old name that was given to Cienfuegos before the Revolución—before many of the city's buildings were bombed and looted during the downfall of Batista. I always liked the name *La Perla del Sur*, because it was beautiful—the Pearl of the South.

In complete contradiction, but much more appropriate, is the name *Cienfuegos*, which means "one hundred fires."

We were married in a small government-owned building called a marriage palace, which was basically a large room where our paperwork was notarized, but it was very special to us. Taire's parents and her sister stood next to us, along with Enier.

Cuban weddings used to be lavish events but were mostly enjoyed by the wealthy. After the Revolución, Catholicism was suppressed, and weddings, which were rooted in Catholic traditions, were discouraged as anticommunist.

As weddings were simplified or bypassed altogether, the importance of marriage also declined. Most couples skipped the pomp and circumstance of a wedding ceremony and simply moved in together. Many of our own friends scoffed at the idea of having a wedding.

But we wanted a ceremony—as unglamorous as it was. We wanted to exchange vows before God and man, and to let the entire world know that I was hers and she was mine.

Our ceremony—if it could even be called such—was very simple, but formal. We both signed our names to the marriage certificate, and my eyes filled with tears. "I love you, Taire. I thank God for you," I said.

I glanced at the notary, who smiled and winked at me as if to say, "Kiss her, you fool!" So that is what I did. I kissed my wife, long and hard, until Enier uncomfortably spoke up: "Take it easy. You are going to suffocate each other!"

We all broke into laughter—including the notary, who

closed her book, handed us our marriage certificate, and said, *"Felicitaciones, Señor y Señora Pereira."* Congratulations, Mr. and Mrs. Pereira. Then she added in a slight whisper, *"Dios te bendiga a ti y a tu familia."* God bless you and your family.

We were taken aback momentarily by the officer's well-wishes, but Enier broke the tension once again.

"Yosely is the only brother I have ever had," he said. "So, I suppose I should welcome Taire to the family. *¡Salud, hermana mía!*" Cheers, my sister!

He then promised to help get her parents and sister back home safely and wished us a happy wedding day. Enier wouldn't let me pay him for their taxi. "It's my gift to you, hermano," he said. And with that, they were gone. Taire and I waved as we watched the taxi disappear behind the pastel-colored buildings that line the downtown streets of the Pearl.

The next day, Taire and I were taken by taxi to Rancho Luna where we spent one night looking up at the stars and walking on the beach—the place where we'd spent our first day together a few months earlier.

Our holiday was short-lived because Taire had to report back to Escuela Mario Castillo in two days. She was a new schoolteacher in Cumanayagua and would be watched very closely during her first few weeks of leading a classroom. On her first day at the school, named for a *Revolucionario* fighter who died a few kilometers from Cumanayagua, an armed policia escorted her from the school's entryway to her room and watched as she welcomed students.

Education is taken very seriously in Cuba, and schoolteachers, under strict scrutiny, must prove themselves worthy of leading a classroom. After all, the future of the Revolución is in their hands.

I hated the fact that Taire was a teacher. I loved her passion for kids and the way she interacted with young children, but being a teacher in a communist country means you are sometimes the first and most meaningful introduction those students will have to the lies of people in power.

Taire was neither a loyalist nor a dissident. Since she was from a rural part of Cuba, her understanding of the government and even the Revolución and its effects on the country was slightly skewed because her family's life on the farm did not change as significantly as most people's. Unlike her uncle Martin, who understood personally the effects of Fidel's stronghold, her father never really took a stance on one side or the other. He was just a farmer who loved to grow trees and share the fruits of his labor with others. Taire had the demeanor of her father but also a curious spirit for learning and teaching. Her intentions were pure. She simply loved being around children and watching them grow. She was born to be a teacher, and I have always loved that about her. It says so much about her heart and her love for others. Part of her role, however, was to teach revolutionary history, and I had a very difficult time accepting that.

The curriculum in primary and secondary schools in Cuba is based on three principles: hard work, self-discipline, and love of country. And by country, the government meant Fidel.

All education is free in Cuba, but not because Fidel was generous. At the end of their secondary education, students pursue either the preuniversity track or technical and professional education. Students who finish preuniversity education receive the *bachillerato*, which sets them apart as potential leaders. Those who finish technical education become either skilled workers or technicians. Education is just another way for the government to separate individuals to serve its best interests.

Taire worked hard for her position, and I always respected her desire to make a difference—to love children and to be an encouragement in the midst of the very real battle between desire and destiny—but it broke my heart to see her fighting alongside the devil.

Taire believed that children possess a light that dims as they grow older. She wanted to be in that light as much as possible, and teaching was her way of doing just that.

She felt more hopeful after a day at school. The days were long and tiring, but she always left feeling energized and longing for more.

Every day was strictly scheduled, but she took great pride in using her creativity to teach art and music. Taire said that was when her students' lights shined brightest.

Even when the children sang politically charged songs about Fidel or Che Guevara, or even "La Bayamesa," the Cuban national anthem, joy filled the room as the children let their voices be heard. Taire also taught her students songs that her father sang to her as a child while tending his trees, and that gave her a very special kind of joy.

Every once in a while, schoolchildren were required to march through the streets in support of the government.

The festivities included creating banners proclaiming allegiance to the Revolución and posters adorned with students' paintings—usually of Fidel or the Cuban flag. I dreaded these parades.

After one parade, I greeted Taire on the front stoop of our home when she came home from school—without my usual smile. "Yosely," she said, stopping me before I could speak, "you know I have to do this. I have no choice. I just can't choose which days to go to school."

"It's wrong, Taire. If you had been through what I have been through . . ."

I reminded her—almost weekly—about the incident with my sister and la policia and how I could never support the government. Evidently, she was tired of it.

"Stop, Yosely! Don't you dare talk down to me about how difficult it was to grow up in Cumanayagua, to see your poor sister dragged through the streets, to watch your family fall apart because of Fidel. Don't do it, Yosely!"

This was the first time she had ever raised her voice at me. I think she was as shocked as I was, but she continued.

"Do you think you are the only one? Don't you understand that we are all living this nightmare? This is what life is, Yosely. This is our home, and we cannot change it!"

"Exactly!" I finally yelled back. "We cannot change it. We cannot change anything! We are slaves, Taire, and you sing songs about them. You parade in the streets, laughing and saying, '¡Viva Fidel!' Long live Fidel! while he is killing us more every day! You cannot do this. You cannot praise this evil anymore!"

I was screaming now, but Taire wasn't backing down. The neighbors were starting to come out of their homes to see what was going on, and she started again.

"What good does it do for anyone to fight them? What choice do we have? You say you cannot support the government, but what about our family? What about our baby? Who is going to support us?"

Baby?

Did she just say baby?!

7

FAMOUS LAND

THERE IS A SILENCE at sea that is hard to explain. When the ocean is flat and you find yourself a million miles from anywhere, there is no sound at all. On several occasions, I panicked and hit the side of the boat with my hand or called out, "Ahhh!" just to make sure I hadn't gone deaf.

For hours at a time, there would be nothing. No talking, no movement whatsoever. My head was heavy, as if someone were covering both of my ears and pressing in as hard as they could. It was a strange sensation to look out on all sides and see nothing but water, and to hear nothing—not even the breathing of the four men sleeping next to me.

My skin was burning. My hands were bleeding. My arms were weak and shaking. My legs were seizing and cramping. My eyes could not focus. The boat felt stuck, as if someone had thrown an anchor overboard.

Panicking again, I thought of my family:

Why am I doing this?

How could I just leave them?

Where are they right now while I'm sweltering in the middle of nowhere?

"Ahhh!" I called out and could barely hear my own voice.

"Ahhh!" I shouted again. This time, it sounded even more distant, as if the screams were coming from beneath the surface of the water.

"Hola!" I called out louder. "Hola!"

"Yosely! What is it?" Javier woke up and looked around frantically.

"Nothing," I said. "Absolutely nothing. We're not moving. We're not going anywhere. What have we done? What have I done? I'm sorry, my friend. I'm so sorry." I began to cry.

"No, Yosely. Don't say that. We're almost there. I just know it," Javier said, picking up an oar and rowing.

The others began to grumble and stir.

"We're almost there, Yosely. I just know it. Remember your family. You cannot give up. Let's go. We're almost there."

Remember my family?

No! I wanted to forget about my family. At that moment, I wished I'd never even had a family. Thinking of them was making this journey all the more excruciating. Without them, I could just stop. I could drop the oar, close my eyes, and simply drift away.

Without them, nothing mattered.

The others started sitting up, one by one. Rafael cleared his throat: "Yosely is right. We're lost. We're nowhere," he said, pushing an oar to the floor of the boat.

"Are we even going in the right direction?" he asked.

I held my head in my hands and with every ounce of breath and energy I could muster, I screamed, "*¿Y mi familia?*"

Where is my family?

And then, with eyes clenched tight, I saw Taire.

She was smiling at me from the kitchen in our home while washing a plate.

You're almost there, she whispered and motioned for me to keep going.

With that, I was suddenly able to see and hear clearly. The questions I had been asking became statements, and once again, my reasons for being on that boat became real.

Mi familia.

"We are going to make it," I snapped back, suddenly appalled at the thought of not reaching our goal. "And we are going north!"

"How do you know, Yosely? The waves can't tell you which direction we're going!" Rafael suddenly found the energy to argue.

"The sun sets in the west!"

I didn't look at him. Instead, I sat upright and pointed aggressively at the sun. "As long as that big yellow ball keeps moving that way—" now exaggerating a point to our left— "we are going north. Now, do you want to fight about the sunset, or are you going to pick up that oar and help get us to America?"

Javier took the oar from my hand, smiled, and told me to take a break. "Rafael and I will paddle for a while," he said, patting my swollen hand. "You need to rest, jefe. You're starting to sound like him," he said, pointing at Rafael, who was still fuming.

"Rest your mind, amigo. We'll follow the sun."

"We could always just look for the brightest star tonight and follow that," Alberto added, now pepped up. "I heard there is a star in the sky that rests directly above Miami, and if we can catch up to it, we will arrive in the United States."

"You want to try and catch a star?"

My tone must have seemed condescending because he quickly shot back, "Never mind. It is just something I heard from my cousin. I didn't say I believed him."

Alberto seemed embarrassed to have suggested such a silly idea.

"No, no. I like it," I said. "Who wants to catch a star?" We all smiled, and my friends began paddling harder as the sun made its way across the sky and to our left.

"*¡Atrapemos la estrella norte!*" Four of us cheered. "Let's catch the North Star!"

* * *

DECEMBER 1997

Taire had a difficult pregnancy with crippling dizzy spells, migraine headaches, vomiting, and dehydration. We had one of the driest rainy seasons in memory and there was not enough clean water in the village.

To make matters worse, the government cut wages across the entire country, so no one had anything extra to pay me for my projects. I worked almost completely for trade.

Creations that I would normally sell for a month's pay I instead had to trade for anything that could give Taire relief: a mango, an orange, a soda, or a stalk of sugarcane.

Taire craved sugarcane. Chewing on cut stalks eased her stomach and even quenched her thirst at times. Sugarcane is usually easy to find throughout Cuba—errant stalks grow on roadsides, in ditches, even in gravel that collects in alleyways—but it was becoming increasingly scarce due to barren markets and the government's control over rations.

People needed sustenance anywhere they could find it.

Taire had to stop teaching as her pregnancy progressed. She spent most of her time sleeping. When she was awake, she had very little energy and found it difficult to even get out of bed. Her mother visited frequently and brought fruit whenever she could, but it was never enough.

One day when I arrived home after another fruitless day of trying to scrape together a few pesos, Taire's mother greeted me at the door. "I'm worried about her, Yosely. She's sleeping all the time and eating very little."

I rushed to the bedroom and found Taire only half-awake, drenched in sweat and moaning. I whispered her name and her eyes opened slightly to meet mine. "*Mi amor.*" My love. She could barely speak these words, but she managed a smile. "Let's have a baby."

Taire said the pain of childbirth was like having her insides twisted and squeezed. It was a deep, internal pulling, like someone was reaching inside, grabbing hold of whatever they could find, and trying to tug it away.

It was the most intense sensation she had ever experienced, but it also felt like an out-of-body experience, like it was happening to someone else. Time had no meaning. Hours passed without any recollection.

She wanted to escape her body and allow whoever was pulling at her intestines to simply take them and let her die.

"Just let me go, Yosely," she cried. "*Déjame morir.*" Let me die.

When she fought the pain, it became worse. When she surrendered to the pain and accepted it, it was more bearable.

I remembered a story she once told me. When she was thirteen, her mother and aunt took Taire to the beach for the first time. She had seen the ocean from a distance but had never touched the water; felt the rush of waves; tasted its bitter, heavy salt; seen its ebb; or wondered where the water went.

She had never learned to swim.

While walking along the water's edge that day, she saw a bright, shining object floating only a few feet away. She walked toward it; perhaps it was treasure—a lost crystal or a diamond, an ancient looking glass or magic lamp.

She had waded waist-deep to retrieve her find, when suddenly a wave crashed over her head and pulled her down. Her back hit the ocean floor so hard, it knocked the breath out of her. She was tossed and tumbled under the water in a roar of confusion. It felt as if something grabbed her ankle and pulled her deeper and deeper until . . .

Silence.

Her body began to float upward. Her mouth was open, and her throat was completely contracted. She felt frozen. She heard her mother's screams, like the bounce of an echo. Then, her body went limp, her mind went blank, and there was peace.

Suddenly, she felt a burst of energy and a burning pain. Taire tried to wave her arms and her legs, but she was stiff and heavy and sinking like a stone.

She woke up on the beach, surrounded by her mother and aunt and a young couple who had been relaxing nearby. The man had dragged her out of the ocean and forced the water from her lungs—like lava oozing from her chest, up through her throat and nose.

Taire regained consciousness and began crying, scared and embarrassed.

That is the closest feeling to childbirth that she could describe, and she felt some sense of relief only when she was screaming at me.

Nineteen excruciating hours later, we welcomed our seven-pound, seven-ounce baby boy.

We named him Orlando, which means, "famous land."

*   *   *

I received a message from my mother a few weeks later saying my sister had escaped. The brief note was scribbled and unemotional: "Yuny left for the United States. She's gone, Yosely."

My heart broke as I read those words. I fell to my knees at the immediate sense of loss, but there was also a strange calm that covered me. My sister was safe for the very first time in her life. She had made it.

Yuny had been working at a cigar factory outside of Cienfuegos, where she met a man named Mikel from the Dominican Republic. The two of them fell deeply in love and were married within just a few weeks.

They had only been married for a few months when her mother-in-law was arrested and imprisoned for practicing religion. Several policia stormed a prayer meeting she was holding in her home, and she was quickly sentenced to twenty years in a Havana prison for women. Yuny's new husband sent word of his mother's capture to relatives living in Miami, who successfully negotiated to have her released to the US government. She was told she could bring her family with her to the United States. Yuny was part of her family now.

This was the first time I ever thought God might actually be real.

8

FISHING EXPEDITION

THE VERY MOMENT I held my son, I felt an immediate and inexplicable connection. What a beautiful creation he was. In his eyes, I saw my eyes. His lips and nose and ears and fingers and tiny toes were all perfectly fashioned.

My boy. My blood.

But it wasn't just the fact that Taire and I had a healthy, handsome son. Suddenly, I had a new purpose. I knew from the moment he drew breath that he was destined for a better place than this.

Everyone on the entire Island seemed to be withering into skeletal versions of their former selves. Everyone except for those who were working with the government—policia, administrators, and even spies—who could not hide their weight, their gluttonous girth.

The rest of us were starving.

Mortality rates among the elderly increased dramatically. The scarcity of basic vitamins left them vulnerable to disease that spread to young and old alike. Babies were dying before their first birthdays.

Food was scarce and hunger rife. For a lot of people,

breakfast was a glass of sugar water at best. Lunch was a mango or an egg. Dinner was whatever you could find, and more often than not, you couldn't find anything.

I remember very clearly counting the days until we were scheduled to pick up the next government ration. Eleven days. Once a month, each citizen was given

five eggs,
two pounds of rice,
one pound of beans,
six ounces of cooking oil,
a loaf of bread,
two chicken breasts, and
sugar.

Before this, the longest I had gone without eating was three days. I knew we wouldn't survive with what we had.

Taire fried our last two eggs on Sunday, and we were saving the remaining bit of rice for Orlando.

In most countries that are labeled "poverty stricken," poor health care, crime, lack of education, or catastrophic circumstances such as drought, famine, or other natural disasters are the accelerators that drive people to desperation.

Not so in Cuba.

Health care is free. Education is required. And crime rates are very low. Common criminals are scarce in Cuba. The fear of being caught doing something illegal far outweighs any natural desire a miscreant might have to lie, cheat, or steal.

But Cuba's poverty is a different breed. A much more sinister and cruel design.

* * *

In the late eighties, when the Soviet Union was preparing to break apart, it put on hold all economic, humanitarian, and military aid to Cuba. The Soviets withheld the expected six billion dollars of annual relief, and our Island faced its direst circumstances in history. This period became known as the "special period," but it was not special.

Not at all.

Despite the almost complete devastation that was being experienced throughout the Island, billboards were erected and propaganda posters plastered even in the most rural areas. They read:

"*¡Jamás doblaremos una rodilla!*" "We will never bend a knee!"

"*¡Viva la revolución!*" "Long live the Revolución!"

"*¡Vamos bien!*" "We are doing well!"

But we were a long way away from doing well. Electricity, coal, gas, and oil were rationed as well as the most basic necessities. Neighbors hoarded food, fearing shortages and famine. In many towns, people became desperate and began eating dogs, cats, mice, and rats and growing vegetables on any patch of ground, even among mounds of human waste and trash.

I feared for the people I loved.

I feared for Orlando.

* * *

There was a river—a glorified creek, really—about three kilometers from the center of town, where lots of large *camarones* (freshwater prawn or shrimp) could be found along the river's edge—under rocks, in small outlets, and in the brush that grew in the water. Camarones can sometimes grow to the size of a small lobster. They are delicious, and they are abundant throughout Cuba.

Rafael, Alberto, and I set out for the river late one Thursday. Alberto had created a few basket traps to catch the camarones without us having to jump in the water.

The traps were made of wire, wood, and plastic. An opening at one end allowed the camarones to enter a funnel of netting that Alberto had created from an old shirt. It was actually an ingenious invention, something someone's father or grandfather had designed a long time ago.

That night, we tied pink strips of plastic to each trap as makeshift buoys that we might be able to see by the light of the stars.

We placed the traps along the river's edge and then sat under the bridge for a few hours, drinking beer and waiting for the traps to fill. When we finally ran out of beer, we walked to the far side of the river and began collecting our bounty. The first two traps contained six or eight camarones, enough to feed each of our families for several days. Rafael took that catch back to our bicycles and waited for Alberto and me to finish checking the remaining traps. By this time, the night sky was pitch-black and it was very difficult to see even one step ahead. Alberto called out, "I have four more, Yosely! The traps worked!"

Just then, I heard a whistle—three short bursts of air. It was a warning. We all knew that if we heard the whistle, something wasn't right. We would stop what we were doing and run in different directions, eventually meeting at my house in town.

The whistle was faint, but true. There was no doubt something was wrong. I quickly reached into the water and grabbed the last trap. It was filled to the top with camarones, heavy and hard to pull. I heard splashing in the water and thought it was Alberto approaching. "Amigo! Go left! Get out of the water! Alberto!"

The splashing stopped. "Hola?" I whispered.

The sudden silence made me nervous. I pulled the trap out of the water and dragged it up the embankment. At the top of the hill, I stuffed the camarones in my shirt and began to run. I had only taken a few short steps when I heard a voice behind me. "Stop, I'll shoot!"

I never heard a gunshot. There was no sound, just a burning pain in my left arm before I even decided to run. The force of the shot swung me completely around and I ended up facedown on the ground.

Almost instantly, my friends were standing over me. "Yosely!" they screamed. "Get up!"

But I couldn't move. I tried to turn, but nothing happened. The darkness around me closed in tighter and tighter until I finally passed out.

Alberto is not a particularly big man, but he's very strong. He picked me up, threw me over his shoulder, and carried me almost one hundred meters to where we had left our bikes.

I'll never fully know how he got me home, but I will forever be grateful.

I had lost almost 40 percent of my blood. My left bicep had been completely separated from the bone in my arm and dangled uselessly at my side. The bullet had ripped through my arm and skimmed my chest, breaking three ribs, but passing through cleanly. By the time we got to my house, both of us were completely covered in blood. I was in and out of consciousness, startling awake then just as quickly blacking out again.

Earlier that day, just after I had left for the creek, Taire's mother delivered a small bushel of pinto beans she and Taire's father had harvested the day before. We hadn't eaten a real meal in a few days, so Taire was excited to be able to cook something the next day.

She was shelling the beans on our front porch when she saw our silhouettes over the incline of the alleyway.

Alberto was screaming over and over, "Get help! He's been shot!" as he carried my nearly lifeless body through the street.

Taire couldn't process what he was saying at first.

He's been shot?

Who?

What does that even mean?

No one shoots anyone else in Cuba.

Nobody has guns!

But then she saw me, completely covered in blood from head to foot. I was moaning when Alberto laid me at her feet, but I couldn't respond to her pleas: "Talk to me, Yosely. Are you okay?" Alberto crawled toward the corner of the house and vomited through deep, gasping breaths.

"What happened?" Taire demanded an answer from someone.

"They shot him for no reason," Alberto said, starting to cry. "They tried to kill us."

He was almost calm as he told the story, never looking Taire in the eye, just staring into the void of the alley as he sat up and leaned against the exterior wall of the house.

"Are you hurt, Alberto? Have you been shot?" Taire asked.

He slowly shook his head, still avoiding her eyes.

When she saw my wound, her knees buckled, and she became weak. She ran to a community phone in the home of a neighbor two streets away and called for help.

Less than an hour later, I was put in the back of a large pickup truck and taken to a medical clinic in Cienfuegos. I was still mostly unconscious when they took me away. Taire thought she might never see me again.

Word spread quickly that someone had been shot by the policia, and the streets began to fill with gossip and accusations. The majority of our friends and family were very upset, but others, knowing I was a dissident, pointed fingers and lashed out with "I told you so" and "He deserves what he gets."

Alberto snapped out of his shock, jumped to his feet, and charged a local who was pointing in his direction and sneering. It took three men to pull my friend off the taunter, but it had taken Alberto only five seconds to break the man's jaw and nose.

"Yosely was trying to feed his family," he sobbed, still being restrained by the small crowd. "They shot him for trying to feed his family."

With that, the men released Alberto and he fell to the ground—like an empty suit folding into itself.

Helping him back to the porch, Taire was met by my father, standing a few feet from the door.

"Is it true? Is Yosely dead?" he asked.

"No! And don't you ever say that again!" Taire cried. "No one say that!" She screamed at no one and everyone at the same time.

"Yosely is not dead! He is going to live! He is going to come back to me."

My father stepped toward her and wrapped his arms around her for the first time since she had known him. "Shhh, *niña. Está bien. Está bien . . .*" he said softly as a single tear ran down his creviced face. Shush, little girl. It's okay. It's okay.

The next morning, our friends pooled their money for Taire to take a cab into Cienfuegos so she could try to find me.

There are only two clinics in the province that take patients who are not associated with the political elite, and I happened to be in the closest one. The building was in almost complete disrepair. A number of ceiling tiles were missing, exposing a complex maze of dripping pipes and cords being held together with duct tape and thin wire.

I was sleeping in a large room that held more than ten patients, all of whom appeared to be in excruciating pain. A few machines beeped and buzzed at the far end of the room.

Taire approached my bedside and gently touched my hand. I was wearing an oxygen mask that fogged with each exhale. Taire began to weep, now knowing that I was alive.

"I love you, mi amor. My Yosely," she whispered and leaned down to kiss my head, which was wet with perspiration. My eyelids struggled to flit open, and a tear streamed down my face when our eyes met.

She sat with me for two days and two sleepless nights before returning home to check on Orlando and prepare the house for my arrival almost three weeks later.

*   *   *

At sea, there is no such thing as an errant storm cloud. It is always the sign of things to come. As the rain started to fall, we tilted our heads and opened our mouths, trying to catch as many drops as we could, and readied ourselves for the impending chaos—hoping and praying this night would not be as terrible as the last.

I held my cupped hands to Neo's mouth so he could lick the drops on my palms. He became increasingly despondent as the water began to swell beneath us and carry us up and down, over and over again.

The winds picked up, and we began to rock back and forth. Suddenly, as if yanked by a great hand, Neo was pulled overboard. He hadn't been holding on, and the force was too great for us to keep him secure.

Instinctively, Rafael dove in after Neo and pulled him to the surface of the raging ocean. Rafael was able to use the force of the next great wave for leverage and hoist our friend back into the boat. The same momentum allowed him to make what looked like a bionic leap over the side to safety. Even he was surprised at the ease with which he leapt out and then back in—as if he had been practicing for that moment all his life.

The impact from the waves slamming each of us up and down and into one another was so great, I feared the boat would splinter.

Neo slinked back down into the hull and covered his head, hiding under the feet of Alberto and Javier. Their stone faces seemed to soften as they looked down on our friend. Something was definitely wrong with him. He just curled up—eyes open, but nothing at all behind them.

We were still being tossed around quite a bit, water rushing in from every direction, accompanied by stinging rain—tiny needles thrusting into our sunburned backs, shoulders, and faces. For hours, the rain came and went, but the sea was constant around us. We didn't know where we were, which direction we were going, or if we were making any progress at all. We just held on as tightly as possible. Rafael and I positioned ourselves in the hull, legs pressed along the side of the boat, creating leverage so we could lock in when we pressed upward on the lip of the boat with our arms. Javier sat in the middle of the makeshift seat, arms outstretched and holding each side. He looked like a boxer preparing to reenter the ring, eyes forward, determined, scowling at his opponent.

Alberto didn't seem to be holding on to anything except Neo. He was leaning over our shaken friend, keeping him close the entire time.

Finally, the winds began to slow and the waves tempered a bit, but the rain continued to pour in torrents, so we all had to focus very carefully on balancing our weight in the unpredictable current.

As soon as the rain slowed, we loosened our grips and relaxed a bit. We were all so tired. So unbelievably tired, too exhausted to speak. I remember looking up at the sky, feeling a cool breeze on my face, and then gazing down at my sleeping friend.

I closed my eyes and quietly asked God to let me sleep.

*　*　*

I was almost completely immobile for the first couple of weeks after being released from the clinic. Taire took great care of me, as did our friends, including my partners in crime Alberto and Rafael, who took turns bringing over extra food.

Enier was particularly helpful, showing us the kind of love that is usually reserved for family. He worked day and night to make extra money or finagle an extra piece of bread or fruit to surprise us every few days. As long as I live, I will never be able to adequately repay him for the kindness he showed to me and my family during that time.

He became my brother.

As I regained some of my strength, I began working a little bit each day, making chair legs, spindles, or cabinet frames that I could use later when someone needed a piece of furniture. My father started showing up every other day or so. He always made it seem like he was just in the area or inexplicably passing by the house, but in reality he was checking on me and Taire and Orlando. It felt good to know he cared.

About a month after I was mostly recovered, my father came to see me again. But this time was different. He was on a mission.

"Yosely, come with me to the shop," he said, motioning for me to follow him. When I walked into the shop, Alberto and Rafael were there too. It turns out the three of them had been conspiring for weeks, and that night they told me they'd identified the officer who shot me.

"It was a young policia named Camilo," Rafael explained. "He lives just outside of town with his brother. He has been bragging about shooting you, Yosely."

"He has to pay," added Alberto.

My father looked at me with tears pooling in his eyes. "This cannot happen again, Yosely. Listen to your friends."

I had never seen such longing from my father. There was an earnestness and desperation in his voice I hadn't heard before. Maybe it was the fact that he was completely sober, but his tone made me stop breathing for a moment before I asked, "What do you mean 'he has to pay,' Alberto? What are you planning?"

I was afraid to hear the answer. That night at the creek had changed Alberto even more than it had changed me. My scars were healing, but his seemed to be much deeper and darker. He looked up at me from under the brim of his hat and then glanced toward Rafael.

"We know where he lives, Yosely. We can visit him. Tonight. We can make sure he never does this again."

"No. Stop." The words left my mouth before I had time to even process what they were suggesting. "I will not hurt anybody. And neither will you. Not for me." I moved toward my friends, who stood up, preparing to hold their ground.

"Yosely," my father interjected, "listen to them. We have a plan."

"You cannot seriously think that I would do something like this! Rafael, look at me! You can't do this." I implored them not to do anything rash.

"What would you have us do, Yosely?" Alberto began to cry. "He almost killed you! I thought you were dead. And for what? They are going to keep doing this to us if we don't stop them."

Rafael turned his back to me and walked to the far side of the workshop. "How can you just sit here and pretend like nothing happened, Yosely? Camilo is a monster. He is laughing about shooting you. He says he hopes to catch you again so he can finish what he started. How can you just sit here?"

A sadness welled up inside me. The same devastation I felt when I watched my sister being dragged through the streets, the same feeling I had when my father was beaten, the same darkness I had spent my entire life trying to escape.

And then it hit me.

"It is illegal to shoot someone—even for the police," I said. "I have witnesses. You two were there that night. Camilo shot me for no reason." My friends turned toward me.

"So, what do we do, Yosely?" Alberto asked.

My father finally broke his silence. "You can press charges. You can send him away. This will be an embarrassment for the government. They'll lock him away!"

"Yes. We can take care of Camilo, but not the way you want to do it," I said. "We will go to the courts tomorrow. It's going to be okay."

I told Taire nothing of our plans. The next morning she had no idea where I had gone as Alberto, Rafael, my father, and I set out for Cienfuegos.

* * *

After the Revolución in Cuba, the practice of law was, well, outlawed, and attorneys were required to reapply to work for the state. Many of them were denied and relegated to work in the sugarcane fields or imprisoned for views contrary to Fidel's. Castro created a law collective called *Bufetes Colectivos*, which were supposed to be nonpartisan representatives of the people, but in Cuba there is no such thing as "for the people."

When we arrived at the courthouse in Cienfuegos—a walk-up storefront where armed officers stood ready, checking papers and manning the door—we were instructed to stand outside on the curb. For more than two hours, the sun burned our skin and we were all very thirsty, but the delay allowed us to quietly continue rehearsing our grievances to the bufetes.

"This is never going to work," Alberto said.

"They're not going to believe you. Let's just go home and pay Camilo a visit."

"If you don't want to be here, you can go," I snapped back. "The only way we are going to get back at Camilo is through the criminals he serves."

I was determined to prove a point to my father and friends, and I was not going to let them get the best of me. I was saving my best for the lawyers.

When it was finally time for me to enter the building, the guard checked my paperwork and slowly read my name: "Yosely Pereira. Yo-se-ly. *¿Por qué estás aquí?*" Why are you here?

"I was shot several weeks ago," I stuttered, unbuttoning my shirt to expose the wounds, still wet with healing. "I almost died, and I would like to see a judge."

The guard turned his head to the side and squinted. "Look at this," he said, motioning for the other guard to investigate the scars. "He says he was shot," he explained, then turned his attention back to me. "Who shot you? Your wife?"

Both of the men laughed, and I could sense my friends' frustration building as they stepped closer to me for support.

"*No su esposa, idiota,*" Alberto grunted. Not his wife, you idiot. "*El estúpido gobierno.*" The stupid government. My friend was looking for a fight, one way or another. The guard on my right stepped forward and held his rifle out like a shield as he pushed past me.

My father stepped between the two men, "*¡Por favor!*" he pleaded. Please! "He is just tired. We have been on the road for a long time. *Por favor, perdónenos. Por favor, perdónenos.*" Please forgive us. Please forgive us.

He must have said those words fifteen times before the guard stepped back, and Alberto angrily turned away to sit on the curb of the tiny road. Rafael, who hadn't said a word to this point, followed him and motioned for me to go inside.

"You go, Yosely. We'll be here if you need us."

The policia smiled and stepped aside. "You can go in now. We'll make sure your friends are safe out here."

My father followed close behind me but was stopped short of the door and told he could not go inside unless he also had a complaint.

"One at a time," the guards said simultaneously. My father disappeared from my view as the two guards closed the gap and faced outward with their rifles clutched tightly against their chests.

Once I was inside, the simple storefront took on a completely different feeling. It was dark inside, and a tiny desk sat in the middle of the spacious hall. A female attendant entered the room and smiled. "Señor Pereira?" I nodded. "How can I help you?"

For the next fifteen minutes, I pleaded my case, describing every second of the night I was shot. I went into great detail about the traps we set and the reasons we were at the creek in the first place. "I have a small child and a wife, and we were very hungry. We were not catching the camarones to sell. We were simply trying to find something to eat."

The bufete listened to every detail, never interrupting me. She took notes and nodded compassionately the entire time.

"So, what is your complaint, señor?" she finally asked.

"The man who shot me is a police officer," I said. "I almost died."

"I see," she responded. Without looking up from her notes, she continued. "And where were you, again, señor?"

"Near a bridge, about three kilometers from Cumanayagua. My friends and I . . ."

She interrupted. "Was this on your property, señor?"

"My property?" I was confused by the question because I had already described my home in Cumanayagua.

"Yes. The place under the bridge. Three kilometers from Cumanayagua. Is this *your* bridge?" Her tone stiffened, and she finally looked up from her notes. "Señor?"

Dejected and suddenly aware of the significance of her question, I whispered, "No."

"No!" She was emphatic now. "You were trespassing, correct?"

I tried to find the words to answer, but she quickly continued, "You were trespassing with two other men, attempting to steal camarones for your family. Tell me, again, Señor Pereira. Why are you here?"

I was a bit taken aback and stumbling over my words, but I tried to explain that even though I was, in essence, trespassing, Camilo had no right to shoot me. But the bufete disagreed.

"Guards!" She called out as if trying to get the attention of a stranger. Three armed policia appeared from the shadows. One of them pointed his rifle at me as they approached. The other two positioned themselves behind me.

"This is Yosely Pereira," the bufete said, "and he is under arrest."

9

WELCOME TO HELL

NOVEMBER 1999

I was taken to prison immediately. My father had to break the news to Taire. He showed up at our door holding three mangoes. Forcing a smile, he said, "I brought these for you and the baby." He paused for what seemed like a full minute before continuing, "Everything is going to be okay, Taire. But . . . Yosely isn't coming home."

He explained that I had been transported to Ariza Prison, an awful place with a reputation for beating, abusing, and cruelly torturing inmates—especially those who were known dissenters.

Ariza was a place parents would often threaten kids with while they were growing up: "If you don't behave, we will send you to Ariza," they'd say. We had never seen the prison before, but it was the place of many nightmares.

Taire was terrified. She had no food. She had no way of making money, and our family's rations were suspended until the government finished their investigation of my trespassing allegation. Not surprisingly, they never finished their investigation.

133

Taire had to be issued a new *libreta de abastecimiento* (a supplies booklet) after being turned away from the local bodega for having an expired ration card. She was forced to travel to Cienfuegos to the *Oficina de Control para la Distribución de los Abastecimientos* (OFICODA), where she was persecuted over and over again for being married to a criminal.

It took begging—literally on her knees—before she was issued a new booklet.

I couldn't contact my family for almost three months. My father visited Ariza many times, but he was always turned away and told that my family would be notified when I was able to have visitors.

During this time, my father, Enier, and others checked on Taire and Orlando, making sure they had enough to eat. Taire began spending a lot of time at her parents' house in Lomitas. They always had plenty of vegetables and milk, and it was nice for her to visit the quiet of home.

I ached for Taire. For Orlando.

What must he think of me? That I deserted him?

Taire became depressed and paranoid. She no longer felt safe and wondered if she would ever see me again. Thirty kilometers away, in a dark, damp jail cell, I was wondering the same thing.

Several weeks after my arrest, Taire became very sick. Her mother was increasingly worried about her and finally arranged for Taire to see a doctor in Cienfuegos. It was a familiar sickness, but Taire couldn't accept her diagnosis. It couldn't be true.

No way.

*   *   *

When I was admitted to the prison, I was labeled a *disidente*, dissident, and treated as if I were a traitor.

In Cuba, a person's loyalty counted above all other qualities. Disloyalty was and still is the unforgivable sin, no matter where you are from or what your role in life might be. I might as well have been planning an overthrow of the government when I reported that I had been shot by Camilo.

I was beaten and kept in what can only be described as a concrete box. The windows were covered with metal, and the guards were forbidden to even look at me. My right hand and left foot were handcuffed together behind my back for the first six days I was there. I was held incommunicado, naked except for a thin gown-like garment that hung, open and torn, from my shoulders.

The way the cuffs were positioned, I was forced to lie on my stomach or on my left side, where the gunshot wound was. The pain was unbearable at times, and I often fell in and out of consciousness without warning.

There wasn't a latrine in the cell, so I had no choice but to writhe in my own excrement. I did not eat for four days in protest before the pains in my stomach from dehydration and hunger outweighed my disgust at the conditions. Tiny bits of bread were sometimes shoved through a slot in the cell door, and I forced myself to swallow them—most soaked with urine or sludge that seemed to ooze through the cinderblock walls.

After the first week, I was moved to a large cell with a ramshackle roof about thirty feet above that leaked and was caved in in certain areas. More than 650 people were spread about the room, in corners or along walls so they would not be hit by the falling debris or soaked by sewage that poured into the center of the room about three times every day.

When a prisoner can't truly live; can't walk around; can't be with his family; can't enjoy ordinary pleasures like listening to music, seeing the sun shine, feeling a breeze, or just seeing the smile of another human being; if he is reduced to the life of a dormant plant waiting for a spring that never comes, he would rather die than simply exist.

I saw three suicides in the first two weeks I was at Ariza, horrible scenes that play out in my mind to this day. But my resolve came from a different place than mere survival. I had Taire. I had Orlando.

And I had the promise of a God who I was starting to trust.

I would not die here.

Not here.

*   *   *

FEBRUARY 2000

Ariza is not a labor camp like I had seen before. Prisoners spent twenty-two hours a day inside, sometimes in solitary confinement, but most often cramped together in a large cinder-block cell, wasting away, awaiting daylight.

After about three months, several of the guards learned I was a carpenter, and they would pull me aside from time to time to repair tables and chairs or make a simple desk or cabinet door. They were very kind to me and would sometimes reward me with a piece of fruit or a leftover slice of bread.

"You're very good, Yosely," one of the guards said one afternoon as he escorted me back to the cell. "Perhaps if you didn't work so fast," he hinted, "we would be forced to keep you overnight to finish your tasks. Maybe you would not be able to return to join the other prisoners."

The thought of not having to sleep on the floor, fighting off rats and other inmates—for even just one night—filled me with such relief that I begged, "Please. I'll do anything you want. Please. Let me keep working. I can make you anything you want."

"Tomorrow," the guard said. "I think I can find some things for you to do in the officers' barracks."

That night I hardly closed my eyes. Anticipating a restful night's sleep was almost more than I could bear. The next morning, my hands were strapped together with a plastic zip tie you might see used to fasten fencing to poles or to secure a sack of coffee, and I was taken off property to a home about thirty minutes north of the prison.

The guards didn't speak to me during the drive. They joked with each other, laughing and smoking cigarettes, but never acknowledged I was in the van. When we pulled into the gravel entryway of our destination, we were met by a beautiful young woman who waved happily and ran to meet us. This was the home of the guard who arranged to bring me here, and the young lady was his very pregnant new bride.

"You will find everything you need in back, Señor Pereira. You have two days." With that, the other guard cut the plastic binding from my wrists and escorted me to a flat, grassy area behind the house where I was told to build a baby's crib.

A SEA BETWEEN US

Brand-new tools—some still in their packaging—were stacked neatly among beautiful pallets of treated timber. I had never seen wood so clean, so perfect.

Without saying a word, I approached the work space and glanced ahead to see the young woman watching and smiling from the doorway. She gave me a quick nod of her head and turned to her husband, who called out, "We'll be watching, Pereira! *Dos días nada más*," he reminded me, and then tipped his cap. Just two days.

I knew building a crib would not take me two days to complete, so I prepared carefully and took my time putting together a plan. I was going to use up and enjoy every second I was permitted to be away from Ariza.

My mind took me to Cumanayagua with Taire. I imagined us sitting on our front porch, watching Orlando play with his figurines. I imagined her smile, her touch. I imagined my boy holding his arms high, begging to be held, and the satisfaction of swooping him up into the air, then holding and hugging him tightly to my chest.

"Do not fear. I am with you always, *hijo mío*." My child.

I don't remember fashioning the slats and spindles for the crib. I cannot recall a single detail of building the bed—the legs, the base, the rounded frame for the headboard, or the hinges that allowed for the broad side of the crib to be raised and lowered. For those two days, I was not a prisoner. I was home.

Suddenly, I felt a hand on my back, and a soft, sweet voice startled me back to reality. "Señor Pereira," the young woman said, "thank you. It's more beautiful than I could have imagined." The soon-to-be new mother was standing next to me,

138

tears streaming down her face. Wiping her cheeks with both hands, she cried, "*Perfecta.*" Perfect.

"You've made my wife very happy," the officer added. "Thank you."

"Is it time to go back?" I asked, anguishing over the answer I was about to receive.

"You will leave soon," he said, "but first, we drink."

With that, he offered me a beer and invited me to sit.

"Your father visited Ariza yesterday," he said. "It seems you have some business you need to attend to in Cumanayagua."

My heart sank.

Cumanayagua.

"My family?"

"Your family is okay," the officer said.

"Well, then, what is it?" I demanded, standing up.

"I could get in very big trouble for what I am about to do," he said. "But I have friends at the prison. They owe me."

I was confused and getting more and more anxious:

What business do I have at home?

Why did my father visit the prison?

Is the guard being honest with me?

What trouble could I bring to him?

"Por favor," I pleaded. "Is my family okay?"

"Finish your beer," he demanded. "Your wife is pregnant, and it's time for you to go home."

Taire is pregnant?

I think I blacked out for a few seconds. Everything went silent, and I sat frozen in disbelief. The guard stood and offered me his hand. "It seems you were a very busy man before you were arrested. Congratulations, señor."

And with a smile, he added, "You know, Señor Pereira, you really are a very good carpenter."

*   *   *

FEBRUARY 10, 2002

I woke with the sun.

The sky was still dark but there were ribbons of color—orange, red, and yellow, and streaks of deep blue. I had seen many sunrises in my life, but this was the most beautiful, the most dreamlike, I had ever been awake for. My throat tightened and I was suddenly overcome with emotion. "Taire," I whispered, and then I began to cry silently. Alone. Cramped in that tiny boat, watching this miracle of color be shaped into day.

Taire loved sunrises and sunsets.

Sometimes when I woke up, Taire would rush in with a great big smile. "Yosely, come look," she would beg. "Isn't it beautiful? Isn't it the most wonderful thing you have ever seen?" I never fully appreciated or understood her fascination with the light breaking through darkness, but in that moment I had no doubt why she loved it so. It was hope. She saw the miracle of hope every day and knew that there was beauty out there. Somewhere.

As the sun burned through the clouds, I thought about the boat. I couldn't help but be proud. Through every storm and the shark attack, and despite being flipped over by walls of water more times than I could recall, the boat had stayed intact. It was a good boat, strong and sound. And it not only kept water from coming through but it also held the rainwater that settled in its hull. For a moment, my father came to mind.

I thought he would be proud of me.

But he would never let me know.

I laughed out loud thinking that he would have been hard-pressed to find something wrong with the boat, but he still would have offered a comment to let me know what he would have done differently.

"The angle of the upper boards should be thirty degrees inward," he'd say, running his hands along the outside. "Don't you know you're having to row harder because the wind cannot pass uninterrupted?" We would already be in America drinking Budweiser and driving Cadillacs if he had built it.

I looked at my friends and smiled. They were still asleep, holding on to one another as if each man were a blanket. We were still nowhere, but we weren't in Cuba. And we weren't alone. Rafael stirred, and when he realized he was snuggled up to Alberto, he shoved him away and quickly looked up to see if I had noticed. I just smiled and shook my head. Alberto groaned and moved even closer to Javier, who was pressed firmly against the side of the boat, his face smashed between the wood and Neo's shoulder.

"How long have you been awake?" Rafael asked me.

"Long enough to have a lot of questions about your relationship with Alberto."

"Stop it right now," he said with an awkward smile.

We both started laughing and I grabbed both sides of the boat, jerking it side to side, and sending Rafael splashing into the water. Alberto and Javier woke to my screams of laughter as I hung over the side of the boat and pointed at Rafael, who was now doing his best backstroke around the vessel. This was the first time I had laughed—really laughed—for as long as I could remember, and it felt good.

Javier and Alberto were confused, but the sight of our friend swimming around us was enough to make them join me in laughter. For a moment or two I forgot we were in the boat and that the previous two days had even happened. I forgot about how thirsty I was, how hungry and tired. I forgot about the sharp pains of dehydration and the paralyzing hunger that was making us lurch and heave and have painful diarrhea. We were just a group of friends on an adventure.

"Neo, you've got to see this! Look at this fool," I shouted and looked back over my left shoulder, hoping our friend had woken up in the same good spirits as the rest of us. "Neo, come look at Rafael."

Nothing. He wasn't moving. I had been so patient with Neo over the past couple of days. I had stood up for him when the others were fed up; I had taken his shifts rowing because he was frozen by fear; I had defended him and kept him safe and close to me, trying to comfort and encourage him during the nights by whispering about old memories and painting a picture of what we could expect when we finally made it to freedom. But I was tired. I was trying to grasp for more grace, but the well was empty. Now I was angry.

"Wake up, Neo, and look at this! I'm not kidding, *imbécil*! Wake up. Now!" Still, no movement. He was incorrigible.

"Javier, wake him up. I'm done with him!" I didn't know if I was angrier at him for ignoring me or for ruining my happy moment, but I could feel my heart pounding, and

I became almost dizzy with rage. I couldn't wait to get to America and be finished babysitting this full-grown infant of a man.

I had turned to watch Alberto pulling Rafael back into the boat when Javier screamed, "Neo!" It wasn't anger in his voice. It was panic. Fear.

The next few hours passed in slow motion. Like a dream. Bits and pieces are clear, but most of what I saw or heard is now muffled or blurred in my memory. Neo was dead.

Javier sat in the bottom of the boat holding Neo's head and weeping. The others pushed past me and rushed to our friend, but I was paralyzed by the sight of him. His face was bloated and gray; his lips pursed and blue; his eyes open and bloodshot. I froze and couldn't catch my breath. I felt like I was watching this grisly scene play out from above the boat. It was as if I had left my own body and was floating above someone else's nightmare. This was happening to them, not me.

Neo had drowned in about two inches of water pooled on the floor of the boat. Like the rest of us, he must have passed out after the storm but landed facedown. We were surrounded by billions upon billions of gallons of raging waters, and Neo had drowned—inside the boat.

This could have only happened to him—my helpless, hapless, homeless old friend.

10

"AHORA ESTAMOS COMPLETOS"

I ENTERED A different kind of prison when I returned home. The policia had their eyes on me at all times. I couldn't walk down the street without being stopped, questioned, or told to go back to my home. Friends in Cumanayagua were warned not to interact with me. I was a pariah, with no way of making money. And even if I had money, I wouldn't be able to buy wood or tools for carpentry. It was illegal to buy them, and sellers were in even more danger of being punished.

For weeks, we had to beg, borrow, and even steal to survive.

Depression is common in Cuba, but I had always prided myself on being above the darkness. I watched up close as my father wasted into despair, and I wasn't about to become a victim. But the unceasing struggle to feed and care for our growing family brought both Taire and me to tears almost every day. Taire cried for our child. Our children.

And I cried for Taire.

Every night, she would stand outside Orlando's door and listen as he whimpered himself to sleep, his stomach never full, always aching for more. The pain of seeing our child suffer was almost too much for her, and now she was pregnant with another.

"I don't know if I can do this, Yosely," she whispered through tears as she leaned against Orlando's door. "I don't think I can bring another child into this home. I'm scared, Yosely."

The only thing I ever wanted for my family was for them to feel safe, protected, cared for, and free—free from worry, free from fear, free from pain.

It broke my heart to see her fight each and every day to smile, to play with Orlando, or to teach him even the most basic things: "*Sí, no, el gato, un perro, uno, dos, tres, cuatro; la vaca dice: 'muuuu.'*" Yes, no, the cat, a dog, one, two, three, four; the cow says, "moooo."

I took her hand and slowly led her to the mattress in our bedroom, where I held her for a while. "Do not be afraid, mi amor," I whispered. "We are going to be safe soon. Very, very soon," I offered again, pulling her forehead to mine. "You can do this, my love. And I will be with you, always."

The words from my tiny prison Bible resounded over and over in my head: *Do not be afraid. Do not be afraid. Do not be afraid.* And they softly echoed through my whispers, over and over again until she drifted to sleep in my arms.

That night, the streets were quiet. No voices of neighbors. No passing cars. No barking dogs or screeches of fighting cats. I sneaked out of the house to a faraway farm on the outskirts of town. The farmer was a friend of my father's, and he raised pigs and chickens for the government.

Farmers and others often resorted to keeping pigs and

chickens, goats, and other animals in their houses because, while the majority of the residents of Cumanayagua were very honest and law-abiding, starvation causes people to disregard morals for something to eat. People like me.

I walked up the long path from the road to the farmhouse and saw no lights on inside. The chicken coop was directly behind the house, so I had to crawl past the front porch, alongside the cactus hedge that lined the yard. Once inside the coop, I froze. *What do I do now?* I was looking for eggs, but then I got greedy. *Who needs eggs when you can have a whole chicken?*

I grabbed the bird closest to the doorway and immediately regretted the decision. It started flapping and flailing and clawing and screeching, and I didn't know what to do. I grabbed it by its feet and took off running through the farmer's field. As fast as my legs would take me, I ran away from the house and the coop, with a terrified chicken flapping for its life. When I was far enough away from the farm, I stopped running, but the chicken kept thrashing. There was no way I could get this bird home without being caught.

I only knew two ways to kill a chicken. The first was to cut off its head, but I was in the middle of a field with no knife, no machete, and certainly no axe.

The second was to wring its neck. My grandmother made it look easy.

But it's not easy.

You have to hold the chicken by the feet and neck—outstretched and straight in front of you. Then you pull down and twist up at the same time. If you feel a snap, the chicken should die within a few seconds.

I had the chicken under my left arm and knew what had to be done. But this chicken was a fighter. She pecked and scratched and flapped around so much that I lost my grip and she jumped from my arms as if in slow motion. I dove after her but missed.

You may never have seen a chicken run before, but it's actually quite impressive. She took off in a zigzag pattern, like an errant kite being pushed by the wind, back in the direction of the farmhouse. I ran after her, diving over and over until I finally snagged a foot and held on like my life depended on it. At that moment, I knew that several lives depended on it, so I didn't let go when the chicken began pecking and biting and clawing at my arms. I sat up quickly, grabbed its feet, ran my hand up its body to the neck and pulled as hard as I could. The chicken's head snapped off completely in my hand and then it began running again in circles until it finally fell over about fifteen meters away.

I knew I would never be able to retell this story to anyone, so I just sat and relished my victory for a few minutes before picking up the finally dead chicken and slowly walking home.

No questions were asked the next morning when we all ate fried chicken for breakfast, but Taire and I smiled knowingly at each other, enjoying every last bite.

* * *

Taire and Orlando visited her parents in Lomitas for a couple of days while I stayed behind to look for supplies so that I could build a few items for a neighbor. I had been promised a package of three light bulbs in exchange for a few cabinets, some shelves, and a new door for the Artegas family.

Freddy Artegas was a known cigar smuggler who was rarely arrested, but when he was, the police usually let him go because he was also their dealer.

It seems, however, that Freddy had become too friendly with an officer's daughter, so Freddy was arrested and his home ransacked by more than twenty policia in a chaotic raid.

No one ever saw Freddy after that night. Rumors scattered that he was being held in Havana, but even his own siblings didn't know for sure.

That raid is why I sent Taire and Orlando away. I was afraid that our house might be next, and I didn't want Orlando around when they came for me.

I had nightmares almost nightly. I awoke thrashing, sweating, and crying out, *"¡Ayúdame! ¡Dios mío! ¡Ayúdame!"* Help me! Dear God! Help me!

My past would visit me at night. Every tragedy. Every heartache. I was scarred, literally and figuratively. I missed Taire beside me. I missed her running her hands along my arms, shoulders, face, and back as I faded off to sleep.

The surface of my skin was like a ridged terrain, my forearms uneven, rutted, and forever bruised from beatings in prison. My hands were hardened, calloused, and indelibly stained with the grime of labor camps. Scars along my biceps and chest were permanent reminders of the nightmares that came and would come again.

I sent Taire and Orlando away because I knew what it was like to see my father beaten and taken away. I knew the horror of looking evil in the eye and watching it win over and over again.

I wouldn't allow that to happen to my son. At any and all costs to myself, I would always protect him.

*　*　*

SEPTEMBER 2000

Our daughter was born on a Wednesday afternoon at Taire's parents' house. Unlike Orlando, she arrived quietly and with a fair amount of ease. There was no drama around her birth; she simply decided it was time to join us, so she swiftly, gracefully entered the world, eyes wide open and full of light.

Yusnay is a name that means "well born," and we couldn't think of a more fitting way to describe this precious breath of heaven.

I had received word that Taire was in labor from a friend of her family, and I dropped everything and began running toward Lomitas, never slowing down.

I bolted through the bedroom door, drenched in sweat, unable to breathe. "Taire! *¿Estás bien?*" I finally stuttered and fell to my knees to crawl closer. Are you okay?

"*¡Mi amor! ¡Mi corazón! ¿Estás bien?*" My love! My heart! Are you okay? I was so concerned with Taire's health, I hadn't even noticed her mother in the corner of the room holding our baby girl.

"I'm fine, Yosely. I'm better than fine," she said, and then pointed toward Yusnay. I began weeping immediately as I reached for her.

"*Gracias, Dios. Gracias. Oh, eres un ángel, mi niña.*" Thank you, God. Thank you. Oh, you're an angel, my little girl. "*Una angelita.*" A little angel.

"*Ahora estamos completos,*" Taire looked at me with tears now streaming.

We are now complete.

*   *   *

I loved watching Taire care for Yusnay and Orlando—so kind and gentle and full of smiles and hope.

But when she was alone, she would cry.

The kids' play area was less than one meter in each direction. Taire took great care in clearing the space of weeds and rocks and trash. Almost every afternoon, she would lean against the front porch and watch Orlando stack or build things with discarded bottle caps and cry.

And then I would watch each night as her spirit seemed to depart her body, leaving a sad, sad shell.

I teetered on the edge of sadness most days too. Nighttime was the worst. That's when I would hear her weep. She was the strongest person I had ever met, but the love she had for our children weakened her resolve. To see and feel and hear her pain was an excruciating helplessness I did not know how to overcome.

Yusnay was unable to breastfeed—something with the enzymes in Taire's milk upset the baby's stomach and caused her to vomit most of what she took in.

The powdered milk she needed was very expensive, and even with the extra pesos I was making with my carpentry, we could only afford a few ounces every month. This was especially difficult for Taire to accept. As a mother with nothing else to offer her child, she felt like a failure, helpless to give the only thing her new baby needed to survive.

At the beginning of every week, I would plead with officials at the clinic in Cienfuegos and Cumanayagua to release more formula for the month. "I will do anything," I said. "I will pay you next week. Please."

The only other option was to admit Yusnay to a clinic where she would be cared for and watched over by government doctors. This was not an option for me or Taire.

I would never let them take our baby.

*　*　*

One afternoon, while walking home from visiting a friend outside of Cumanayagua, I saw a child's bicycle discarded in a pond. The pond was covered in algae and smelled of excrement, but I waded into the water and retrieved it from the slop. It had evidently been run over by a vehicle and left for scrap metal. The frame was slightly bent, the handlebars were askew, and the front tire was flat, but I knew that I had the tools and the determination to make it rideable again. I quickly took the bicycle home and got to work with a tire iron and rubber mallet.

"Yosely, where did you get that bicycle?" Taire asked as she stood in the doorway of my shop. Her question startled me, and I snapped back, "None of your business, Taire! Go back inside!"

She was stunned and hurt by my tone. I never raised my

voice—especially at her. "Fine!" she said. "I'll just leave you with your new toy then."

Then, she added, "¡Niña!" Infuriated by my reaction, she turned and rushed back into the house.

Truth is, I was embarrassed about the bicycle. Embarrassed about what I was going to do.

A few minutes passed, and after walking back to the house, I sheepishly reached my hand around the corner of our bedroom door, holding a marabou flower.

Like a scared puppy still wagging its tail, I approached Taire.

"Get that hideous thing away from me," she said, giggling. I inched closer and joined her on the bed.

We sat there for a minute or two—me holding the flower and she feigning anger—and then we started laughing like a couple of children. I took a deep breath.

"I'm sorry, Taire. I just wanted it to be a surprise."

"You wanted what to be a surprise? The bicycle?"

"No. You'll see, mi amor. You'll see tomorrow." Standing up, I grabbed her hand and helped her to her feet. "We're going to get out of here one day, Taire. But first, I need to sell my shoes."

* * *

I had a new pair of boots—new to me anyway—that were given to me by an old man who couldn't afford to pay for the table I had made for him. Oftentimes, I would accept a trade for my work because very few people in Cumanayagua could afford the luxury of the new furniture or tools I created for them in my shop.

The boots had been made in the United States and were constructed of thick leather with laces up over the ankle, like military boots the soldiers wore in big cities. I could tell they were very expensive, unlike any footwear that could be found in our town.

My idea was to create a lottery of sorts. Instead of trying to sell the boots on the black market, where I was sure to get only a few pesos for them, I would go throughout Cumanayagua showing passersby my beautiful, new leather boots and sell each willing individual a ticket that gave them a chance to win the boots. I would charge a peso per ticket.

In order to cover more ground and invite more people to join the contest, I needed a bicycle. I tried borrowing a bicycle from friends and neighbors, but no one was willing to part with theirs. So when I saw the small, bent bicycle, I was thrilled.

That night, I pieced together a less-than-admirable, but better-than-walking means of transportation to begin my campaign.

The next morning, I pedaled the ramshackle bicycle for what seemed like hundreds of kilometers, blanketing the entire city of Cumanayagua and the valley surrounding it with numbered pieces of paper and the promise that "*Por solo cinco centavos . . .*" For just five cents, "you could own these boots from the United States!"

I sold more than three hundred tickets that day, making enough pesos to buy an entire month's worth of formula for Yusnay.

At the drawing two days later, a drinking buddy of my father's was the winner. He ended up trading the boots for a two-dollar bottle of rum, a prize worth ten times less than the powdered milk we needed for our child.

Taire couldn't believe what I had done. When I arrived back home, she rummaged through our entire house looking for other things to sell off. "Here! Take this," she exclaimed, holding up the dress she wore at our wedding. "Get on your little bicycle and see what you can get for this!"

When she looked up and saw me, eyes wide and stunned at how excited she was, she quickly realized she was acting like a maniac and started to laugh. We both did. And then we fell asleep holding one another.

That was a good day.

* * *

I examined Neo's body like it was a treasure map. I was looking for a clue. *Why did this happen? How? He was alive when we went to sleep. I didn't hear anything or see anything. Did he suffer? Could I have saved him?*

I didn't even realize I was talking out loud until Alberto pulled me from my daze. "There is no reason. It just happened. Death is a part of life, Yosely." He spoke to me matter-of-factly, as if he had rehearsed his lines. "But at least he didn't die alone," he said. "At least he didn't die back there." He motioned behind us and began to weep. "He died on the way to freedom, which is more than I can say for the rest of us if we don't keep going."

Rafael wiped his face and agreed. "We are getting closer, Yosely. I just know it. We have to keep going."

"Of course we are going to keep going!" I insisted. "And

we are going to make it." Looking down at my old friend, I began crying too.

"What about him?" Javier was stroking Neo's cheek and looking into his face like a doting mother caressing a sleeping child. "What are we going to do with Neo?"

I looked up, not sure I'd heard him correctly. "What do you mean, what are we going to do with him?"

"Yosely," Alberto said quietly as he grabbed my hand. "Neo is gone. We have to . . ." He couldn't bring himself to say the words, but I knew what he was suggesting.

"No!" I screamed and stood straight up in the boat.

"Yosely! Be careful!" Rafael moved close and tried to pull me down by my arm.

"Yosely," Alberto demanded, "we can't arrive in the United States with a dead body."

"This is not a dead body!" I screamed and began weeping. "This is our friend! This is our brother!"

"Yosely, please." Javier took his eyes off Neo and urged me to sit. "They're right. We could be put in prison or worse! We cannot take him with us."

It was as if the three of them had already anticipated this scenario and agreed on what to do before we'd even left Nazabal. I couldn't believe what they were suggesting. My legs became weak and I collapsed to my seat. Staring into the great void behind them, I became nauseated and began heaving, my body trying to vomit, but I had nothing to release.

I started crying and fell backward, staring at the clouds moving slowly above.

When I closed my eyes, I saw Neo. I saw his face, his smile, his big green eyes. He was standing on the edge of the ravine making jokes while I built our boat. He was laughing. He was riding his bicycle, taunting the policia. He was dancing. He was gathering supplies for our journey. He was celebrating as we put the boat in the water.

He was happy.

He had hope.

11

FINALLY

There was a small orchard hidden in a tiny valley outside of town, where Taire and I sometimes went with the kids to eat oranges, a place to step outside the shadows at home. It was a beautiful spot with tall grass that swayed like waves in the wind. At the edge of the field, a small creek split the valley like a splintered crack through a pane of glass.

The various shades of green in this place always amazed me—ranging from the near black of rocks covered in moss, to the most vibrant neon of tiny blades of grass near the water's edge. The sun seemed brighter here too, the way it danced through the shadows of the leaves. Three or four trees yielded just enough fruit for a light snack before we walked home, but it was always enough to make us forget ourselves for a moment or two. While Orlando chased butterflies and dragonflies and pointed in awe at the different birds who also seemed to find solace here, Taire and I would watch and smile.

One afternoon, after a brief but much-needed getaway, we came upon a bicycle accident. Witnesses said that a government truck carrying ten to twelve soldiers or policia had veered too close to the edge of the road, where an elderly lady was biking. She careened off the path into a deep ditch, where she hit her head and remained facedown and still. Too still.

I recognized the lady. It was Señora Cortez, a neighbor of mine when I was growing up. The sight of her lying in that ditch made me angry and sad, emotions I hadn't allowed myself to feel for a long time. I screamed instinctively and ran down the hill to where she lay in the muck.

"Yosely!" Taire shouted at me and grabbed the back of Orlando's shirt to keep him from following me. As she held Yusnay close to her breast, she cried, "Yosely, no! You can get in trouble!"

Taire knew that the first person to arrive at an accident—especially involving a vehicle, and most especially a government vehicle—would be taken in by authorities and questioned. But I couldn't leave Señora Cortez there. Other people were standing at the top of the incline, whimpering and covering their mouths in shock. When I got to the ditch, I stooped down and gently turned her body over, pushing back her hair and wiping the blood from her face.

Señora Cortez was one of the kindest, gentlest humans I had ever met. She made candy at her home—not to sell, but to give to children on their way home from school each day. We called her "Caramelo." She would make the simple candy in a small copper pot over an open flame near her porch. Each morning, she would start a fire inside of a discarded oil drum, where she and neighbors would burn trash or cook throughout the day.

I often watched her slowly stir the white sugar, corn syrup, and water together, never stopping as the sugar dissolved and the mixture began to boil. Then with a wooden spoon, she would test for readiness by drizzling a tiny bit of the mixture into a cup of water, where the lava-like drops would become threads of hardened candy.

If we were lucky, Caramelo would add a mint leaf, orange peel, or vanilla or cinnamon extract to flavor the candy, but most often, she would pour the unflavored mixture onto a small pan. When it hardened, Caramelo would break it into bite-sized pieces, ready to be handed out at 5:00 p.m. when we were released from school. It was our reward for another day of learning.

"*¿Qué aprendiste en la escuela hoy?*" Caramelo always asked me. What did you learn in school today? And then she would smile a big, toothless grin and ruffle my hair or pinch my cheek.

She was one of the very few lights that could outshine the darkness of our day-to-day reality in Cumanayagua. And now she lay lifeless. I held her close for about a half hour until authorities came to retrieve her body and escort me to the police station. I was detained for several hours without being asked a single question. The officers just made me sit there while they completed the report, distorting the facts of the accident to verify just that: it was an accident.

The old lady must have lost her balance and then fallen down the hill. Case closed. One less person to feed every month.

Not even looking up from his paperwork, one of the officers grunted, "You can go now, Señor Pereira. Try not to kill anybody else on your way home." Several of the other officers erupted in laughter as they escorted me out of the station.

I was so tired. I had been living this nightmare for far too long. I held back the tears, fearing that if I allowed just one to fall, it might break the dam that secured the hate I held inside. Something had to change. I could not continue to live this way. I could not allow my family to live this way. I needed a plan.

*　*　*

As accomplished a carpenter as my father was, he could just as easily have been a toymaker. The way he could make wood come to life for the children in Cumanyagua was Geppetto-like.

He never made toys for me or Yuny because he was too busy making them for others. But many nights I would watch him create figurines, toy cars or trucks, or a variety of animals—horses, cows, monkeys, alligators, and birds. And boats.

He crafted small wooden rowboats that little boys would race in creeks, ponds, and even sewage streams that ran downhill. The boats were no longer than twelve inches, and a quarter of that wide, but they were beautiful—exact replicas of the boats I had seen near Playa Rancho Luna, where my mother and her sisters had taken me when I was very young.

There is a meandering road near La Campana, on the way to Playa Rancho Luna, that seems to split the earth in half—separating the lush green and floral of the valley from the plowman's canvas of furrowed brown. After ten or twelve or maybe a hundred kilometers, it seems, the road rises and then bends to reveal the sea.

I remember seeing the sea for the first time and gasping at

its glory. From the road's high vantage point, I could see the bend in the earth, and I knew that forever was just beyond the curved line of the water.

On the beach, my mother and aunts allowed me to put my feet in the water while they scoured the rocks for sea glass. The tiny beachfront at Rancho Luna sits in a cove, where the waves relentlessly churn broken bottles, dishes, and debris from shipwrecks until all the sharp edges are rounded. The slick, worn glass becomes naturally frosted, creating beautiful pieces of tiny art in blues, greens, whites, and translucent browns.

As the ladies filled their shirts with the glass, I was mesmerized by the empty fishing boats, anchored but rocking furiously beyond the cove. They were simple yet somehow beautiful as they danced on the water, back and forth, up and down, over and over again.

Somehow, my father was able to replicate that beauty in the toy boats he created. He very carefully fitted the pieces together as if he were breathing life into the scraps of wood— using no molds or patterns, just two side panels that dovetailed into two bottom panels.

He was meticulous with every detail. "The measurements have to be perfect, Yosely," he'd say. "Otherwise, the boat will not sail in a straight line."

After soaking the panels in a bucket of water and linseed oil, he would begin to bend the wood ever so slightly, until each piece fit perfectly into the next. Each joint would then be painted lightly with molten tar that he boiled over an old oil drum in the corner of his shed.

My father had buckets full of small rock-sized pieces of

dried tar he had picked up alongside the road—shards of tar from sloppy government roadwork. The buckets were hidden under a workbench, a bounty of dirty, stolen jewels.

The bottom of each boat would be coated with tar as well. "I do not build sinking boats, Yosely," he'd say.

It was his example and years of watching him craft hundreds of tiny vessels that gave me the confidence to keep going. *I do not build sinking boats either, Papá,* I thought to myself as I raced through the alleyway to meet Enier.

I finally had a plan.

* * *

Orlando and Yusnay shared a tiny space separated by a half wall that I built in our bedroom. I elevated a small mattress with wooden blocks in the corner of the room for Orlando's bed, closed in by Yusnay's crib. There was no room for a bed frame in the space, but the blocks kept the mattress away from moisture and rodents.

My daughter's crib was a work of art, if I do say so myself. I had weaved together light and dark woods into an almost impossible pattern. The wood was stitched together, like a tapestry hanging in a museum, each piece bending and weaving in and out, each tiny spindle and the frame polished until it shone.

Taire marveled at the crib. I think that was the first time she realized how much I loved working with wood. It was then, too, that my relationship with my father took on new meaning for her.

She saw the longing there, an emptiness I worked hard to

fill. I wanted my father to be proud of me, to see and know his son the way I saw Orlando.

When I wasn't home by his bedtime, Orlando would ask for his *papá*. He wanted a story or a back rub. He would cry himself to sleep when I wasn't there.

It made me proud to be wanted, but it anguished me to be missed.

Upon arriving home, I would curl up next to my boy and whisper as we fell asleep:

"*Siempre estoy contigo.*" I am with you always. "*No tengas miedo.*" Do not be afraid. "*No tengas miedo.*"

Taire noticed something change in me after Señora Cortez's death. She didn't know what, exactly, but something was definitely different. I was gone more—most days, I left before the sun rose, and sometimes I came home in the middle of the night.

* * *

Our neighbor Luisa was a know-it-all. She was rude, nosy, unpleasant, unlovely. I often wondered if she really was that awful or if she was just a great actress.

But nobody is that great of an actress.

When Luisa noticed I wasn't around as much as usual, she decided to investigate.

"Taire, where is your husband?" She stuck her head in our window and looked around as if she was "it" in a game of hide-and-seek. "Where is he? I need to speak with him."

"*Discúlpame, por favor, Luisa.*" Excuse me, please, Luisa. "What business do you have with Yosely?" Taire answered.

Luisa always had her nose—and sometimes a few other things—in other people's business, and now she quite literally had her nose in Taire's.

The joke in our barrio was that Luisa must be a spy for the government the way she interrogated everyone, but I don't think there was anything covert about her nosiness. She had no husband and no job, but always had plenty to eat and even bottled water from time to time. I was certain she traded information for food. And if there was no information to give, she would simply use her buxom figure to wheedle a balanced meal. It was no secret that she spent most of her nights lying with various policia, returning home at dawn to get her children ready for school.

"Business? No business," she said. "But he has certainly been very busy lately, hasn't he? He must be doing very well to leave you and the children alone so much."

Taire wanted to scream and knock the judgmental grin right off Luisa's face, but she knew an even better way to shut her up.

"I'm not sure," she said. "Perhaps you should ask his girl-friend how he is doing."

With that, she shooed Luisa's gaping mouth from the window and pulled the curtain. The look on Luisa's face was worth any explaining Taire would have to do later after Luisa told the entire town that I was a two-timer.

Luisa's question did raise Taire's curiosity, though. She often asked me where I had been. My answer was always the same: "I'm taking care of our family. Trust me." And she did trust me.

God only knows why, but she did.

* * *

Alberto shook me softly. I opened my eyes to find his face a few inches from mine. "I think you passed out," he said quietly. "Hermano, we need to say goodbye. It has to be done." I sat up and saw that Rafael and Javier were quickly removing Neo's clothing. As if unwrapping a bushel of sugarcane, they worked aggressively, tearing his shirt and pulling his pant legs off one at a time.

When Neo was completely stripped, my two friends looked at me.

They were right. How could we possibly explain what had happened? We didn't even understand. I nodded, but then added, "*No puedo,*" I can't, and I turned away. The boat rocked slightly as they lifted Neo's body up and over the edge.

The sound of him hitting the water sent a wave of nausea and cold chills through my body. I didn't look back. I just grabbed an oar and started rowing: left, left, right, right, left, left. I paddled slowly at first, but then adrenaline took over and I rowed faster and faster until I felt the surge of momentum carrying us away.

The others leaned over the sides of the boat and began slapping the water with their hands, pushing the water behind us—the four of us now working harder than ever to reach our destination.

Hours passed without a word spoken. The only sounds were the grunts and groans of desperation. Suddenly, I saw a bird flying overhead. Then another. And another.

"Stop!" I yelled, continuing to look upward. "Look." The

others stopped their splashing. "*Gaviotas*," I said, trying to catch my breath. Seagulls. A swarm of seagulls and pelicans were flying overhead, which could only mean that we were close. Right?

"Listen!" Javier whispered, and then we all heard it. A boat's engine getting louder. We all froze as if being completely still might make us invisible to the coast guard. We had all heard stories of refugees getting close to America's shores, only to be intercepted by US authorities and forced to return to Cuba.

"Yosely?" Javier broke the silence. "Yosely, what do we do?" I wanted to offer a solution, but what could we do? We couldn't hide. We couldn't swim away. We couldn't outpaddle a ship's propeller.

Alberto stood up. "I will not go back to Cuba. They'll have to shoot me first." Rafael agreed, and the two of them seemed to be preparing to fight. Then we saw it. A small boat was approaching, and the captain seemed to be waving to us, moving his arms back and forth above his head.

"*¡Hola!*" We heard his yelling but still couldn't see his face. "*¡Hola!*" He called out again and then seemed to turn away from his straight line, finally positioning his boat to pull alongside us. Alberto stood again, pushing out his chest, and scowled at the man behind the steering wheel.

He was an American. And he was alone.

"*¡Hola, amigos!*" Hello, friends! A great big, toothless smile came across his face, which was covered in a long white beard. "*¿Hablan inglés?*" Do you speak English?

The four of us looked at each other, unsure of what to do

or say. Javier was the only one of us who spoke any English, and he knew very little.

"I speak English," he said. "*Un poquito.*" A little bit.

The American told Javier that he was a fisherman. "You're headed in the right direction," he said with a smile. "You're almost there!" Javier asked if he could take us the rest of the way.

"I could get in a world of trouble if I do that," he said apologetically, "but you're almost there. You can do it."

Javier explained that we had been at sea for three days without water. The man rushed below the deck of his boat and returned with four bottles of water, two beers, and three ham sandwiches, which he tossed to us.

His gifts were gone in a matter of seconds. "Bless your hearts," he said. "Now, you'd best get going. It'll be getting dark in a couple of hours."

"*¡Vayan con Dios, amigos!*" he called out and then pointed ahead of us. Go with God, friends! "You're almost there," he said again. "*¡Bienvenidos a los Estados Unidos!*" Welcome to the United States! And with that, he sped away, looking back at us and motioning for us to keep going.

"You're almost there!" The faint echo of his voice finally reached us as he disappeared over the southern horizon, and we began rowing again.

Faster than ever.

The others saw the shore first. My head was down, and I was using every ounce of strength I could gather to reach out and grab the water with my oar and then pull it back, over and over again.

"*¡Veo tierra!*" Rafael screamed. I see land!

My friends began shouting and crying and hugging each other. Alberto jumped in the water and started to swim. The others were about to join him, but I held them back.

"Alberto! Get back in the boat. We're not safe until we can touch land."

"What do you mean?" He kept swimming. "We made it!"

In the excitement, the others had forgotten that a Cuban who was caught or captured on or in the water would be sent home, imprisoned, or shipped to another country, but if we could just make it to shore—to the sand, to dry land—we would be allowed to stay.

Suddenly, Alberto remembered this law, and leapt back into the boat as if he were in boiling water.

We rowed and we rowed and we rowed until the tide began to break beneath us and push us further in. About twenty meters from the shore, we all abandoned the boat and dove in.

The waves knocked us down as we tried to run through the surf, so we crawled, slapping at the water and flailing toward shore. My arms and legs and lungs and eyes were burning. My head was spinning.

My heart was about to explode.

And then finally . . .

Rest.

The sand was hot and gritty on my face as the tide washed over me and pulled back again. I heard the others splashing at the water's edge—crying and celebrating—but I couldn't move. I lay there, exhausted, in shock. *Am I dreaming? Did we really make it? Was I free? What now?*

Through a haze I saw a pair of bare feet running toward me. "*¡Yosely, ahí vienen! ¡Vienen por nosotros! ¡Levántate!*" Yosely, they're coming! They're coming for us! Get up! My friends were screaming, urging me to move. Rafael grabbed my arm and started to pull, but I just lay there, softly repeating to myself, *Do not be afraid. Do not be afraid. Do not be afraid.*

A woman's voice called out. "Wait! Wait! Don't run. You're safe. Wait!" Rafael gently helped me sit up. Leaning on my elbow, I wiped the salt and sand from my eyes and saw the woman walking cautiously toward us, as if she were trying to calm an agitated animal, her hand outstretched, inching closer and closer.

"Shh, shh, shh . . . it's okay. You're safe. You're okay." We must have looked like four frightened dogs, bunched together, hunched down.

"*¿Estados Unidos?*" I asked. Is this the United States?

"*Sí.* Yes. You are in the United States. You're safe here."

The four of us huddled together, locked arms, and wept. The American started crying too and then pointed back out to sea. "Your boat!" she shouted. "It's floating away!"

Javier got up and ran to the water's edge and yelled, "*¡Adiós, barco! ¡Eres libre!*" Goodbye, boat! You're free! Our crying turned to laughter as we waited for the authorities to arrive.

12

A NEW WORLD

OVER THE NEXT few days, the police knocked on Taire's door four different times. They said they were looking for me, but they knew I was already gone.

Luisa had been very busy, it seems. She overheard Taire and Enier talking that first morning and scampered directly to the authorities with her news.

Taire was questioned over and over about where I might have gone, who I was with, and how I had managed to disappear.

She was upset with me for leaving. She was scared and mourning, feeling abandoned and somehow cheated.

How could he not have talked with me about this?

Why didn't he say something?

Was he safe?

Was he finally free?

It wasn't until she had angrily answered the police with "I don't know!" for what seemed like the hundredth time that it struck her: I hadn't told her because I needed her ignorance to be true.

I betrayed her to protect her.

*   *   *

We were given bottled water, blankets, and granola bars by the American police. They were very serious, but kind. They spoke Spanish and asked a lot of questions before leading us to a large white van that would carry us north to Miami.

How are you feeling?

Where are you from?

When did you leave Cuba?

Are you hurt?

Are you sick?

How old are you?

Do you have family in the United States?

Do you have family in Cuba?

What is your occupation?

These were all very easy questions to answer, but none of us were confident that our answers would suffice.

If I tell them the truth about my family, will they send me back?

If I tell them that my sister, Yuny, now lives in Tennessee, will they send her back?

For the most part, we all kept silent. I just kept answering, "*Busco asilo en los Estados Unidos.*" I seek asylum in the United States. "*Quiero asilo.*" I want asylum.

"*Estás seguro. Todo quedará bien.*" The officers repeated, "You are safe. Everything is going to be okay."

We were taken to Krome Detention Center in Miami. Krome is similar to a military barrack, where detainees live in large pods, housing about fifty detainees each. The pods are not jail cells—certainly not like anything I had ever experienced. In fact, the facility had televisions, large sofas, chairs, and machines that would deliver cold sodas with the simple push of a button.

As soon as we arrived, we showered, then were examined by a doctor who checked our ears, eyes, mouths, and reflexes. He then examined and bandaged our blistered hands and led us to a cafeteria where we were given pizza, fruit, potato chips, chocolate chip cookies, and our choice of drink.

"*¿Tienen cerveza?*" Alberto asked one of the ladies who was serving food. Do you have beer? She lowered her head a bit and raised her eyebrows as if to say, "Don't push your luck, *idiota.*" Rafael slapped Alberto on the arm and pressed him to keep walking.

"It was worth a try," he said. "They have everything else in this place!"

He was right. This was the nicest place any of us had ever been. It was clean and smelled of disinfectant and warm food. I remember thinking that if this is how they treat prisoners in America, I might actually try to commit a crime.

As I sat with my friends and ate the best meal of my life, I thought about Taire.

Is she okay?

Does she understand?

Will she ever forgive me for leaving?

Does she know that nothing is going to stop me from helping her get free?

We were interviewed and questioned for more than three hours before being officially booked into Krome. "The next step is to contact your relatives here in the States," the officer said. "Follow me."

I was taken to a brightly lit, circular room with black telephones along the wall. "Señor Pereira? We have your sister on the phone," the guard said, motioning to a receiver dangling from a spiral cord. "Please keep your conversation short. You will be able to call again tomorrow."

I froze.

Is this call going to be recorded? Is this safe? Am I really about to talk to Yuny? Is this a joke or a trap?

I picked up the receiver and shakily put it to my ear.

"*¿Bueno?*" Hello?

"Yosely!"

It was her. My baby sister. It was really her, and as her voice burst through the line I almost fell to my knees. "Yosely! It's me. Oh, my brother. Thank God. You're free."

I began crying immediately. I couldn't speak. I just wept, as if my soul had been longing for that voice, any voice, to say those words: *Thank God. You're free.*

You're free.

"Yosely. You are coming to Tennessee. You are coming to stay with me!"

I still couldn't speak. I didn't understand what Yuny was saying, and it suddenly hit me that I didn't have a plan. I'd never thought past those words: *You're free.*

Maybe I never really believed I would make it, but that instant was the first time I'd imagined anything beyond the beach where I held the sand in my hands and knew I was in America.

"Yosely? Are you there? Yosely, can you hear me?" Yuny pressed for me to respond, but I simply said: "*Mi familia.* Taire . . ."

"Yes, of course," she said. "We will talk to Taire. I will let her know you are okay. I will send a message." I instructed her to call the gas station in Cumanayagua and speak with Enier. He would be able to tell Taire that I was okay.

The guards at Krome were very kind. They allowed me to talk with Yuny for over an hour. Mostly we just cried, but I made her promise to get in touch with Enier. Before our conversation ended, Yuny said, "I love you, Yosely. Welcome home."

I took a deep breath and told her I looked forward to seeing her in a couple of days, but that I was not yet home.

"Not until I am with Taire," I said, and then I gently hung up the phone.

After the call, I wanted nothing more than to sleep. My thoughts were jumbled and my head ached to the point of nausea. Every sound was harsh and every flash of bright color excruciating. The facility was air-conditioned, a luxury none of us had ever experienced in Cuba, and I began shaking uncontrollably. I wrapped myself in a large wool blanket and lay down on a bed next to my friends, who were also shivering.

I had never considered sleep to be a safe place, but that night, I prayed to be taken there quickly. I was so very tired. As I drifted away, I became a child again. I dreamed of good things. Things of my past: My mother. My father. Yuny. Neo.

I also dreamed of the present—oh, that it could be so. Holding Taire's hand; watching her work in the kitchen, play with our children, and walk slowly through the orange orchard; feeling her arms around me on a motorcycle ride. I dreamed of her eyes, and they were smiling.

For those few hours, by God's grace, I was whole again.

* * *

Washing machines are very rare in Cuba. Only the most affluent and connected residents have enough money to buy machines to wash clothes, sheets, towels, and diapers.

Oh, the diapers.

Every morning, Taire would take our dirty laundry— including soiled diapers—to the kitchen and scrub the filth into our concrete sink using a washboard and leftover water collected from the shower drain.

Soap is very expensive in Cuba, so sometimes Taire would add flower petals or soda ash to the sink to help remove the stench of feces or sweat from a hard day's work. This was a daily routine.

"You do too much, Taire," I would say. "Soon, you will not have to spend your mornings in a kitchen sewer. Soon, you will be able to push a button, sit back, and rest all day."

I always promised things like this. I wanted so badly for her to be able to be lazy.

"One day, we will both be fat and happy." I laughed.

Just before Yusnay was born, I traded carpentry services for a simple electric clothes washer that had a very small agitator compartment and a simple spin chamber. The machine—if you could even call it that—was about three feet tall and no bigger around than two milk buckets side by side.

It was nothing glamorous even by Cuban standards, but Taire said it was the most special gift I had ever given her.

She said anyone who has ever hand-washed a bedsheet, scrubbed baby diapers and hand towels on a washboard next to an electric hot plate in the kitchen, or tried to wring out a pair of jeans to hang on a clothesline in the yard would understand the thoughtfulness of this gift.

She was standing at that machine, watching our children's clothes move around in the murky water, when suddenly Enier appeared from behind the door.

"Psst," he whispered, startling her and Yusnay, who was resting on the ground at her feet. "I told you we would hear something soon," he said, beginning to cry. "Our friend is safe. Our friend is okay."

Enier fell to his knees and hugged Taire around the waist, weeping. Her knees almost buckled, and she slowly knelt beside him.

She grabbed Enier's face in her hands and lifted his chin to meet her eyes: "You talked to him? He's alive?" she asked, tilting her head as if to get a better read.

Enier squeezed his eyes tight and tears streamed down his cheeks.

"Yuny called me. He made it, Taire. Yosely is free."

They huddled on the ground and hugged each other, calling for Orlando to join them in their quiet celebration.

"*Llegó. Gloria a Dios. Gloria a Dios.*" He made it. Glory to God. Glory to God.

* * *

FEBRUARY 13, 2002

After thirty-six hours at the Krome Detention Center, I was taken to a large closet in the rear of the facility that was full of clothing—more shirts and blue jeans and shoes and luggage than I had ever seen. I was met by an elderly nun who smiled as soon as she saw me. She spoke with a familiar accent, and I knew that she was also Cuban.

"You can have anything in the closet that fits you," she said kindly. "You are going to Tennessee tomorrow and you will need a few things." I was embarrassed looking though the clothes, so I paid very little attention to sizes or fabrics. I just picked a few things and waited for her to nod and let me know it was okay.

"You're going to need something with sleeves," she said, pulling a lightweight jacket from its hanger and placing it across my arms, now full of random shirts and shorts.

I looked down and saw a pair of red athletic shoes in the corner of the room. I had never seen anything like them before and couldn't take my eyes off them. They were bright red with white and black soles. Along each side of the shoe was a blue check mark. She leaned down to pick them up.

"Nike," she said. "Good choice."

As she helped me put my new clothes in a large, plastic garbage bag, she told me her story.

Indeed, she was from Cuba. In fact, she grew up less than thirty kilometers from Cumanayagua, where her father was once a politician working for Fulgencio Batista before the Revolución. She was now a US citizen and had been helping refugees reach their families for more than twenty years since the Mariel Boatlift.

In 1980, the economy in Cuba hit an all-time low. People were literally starving to death in the streets. A large group of brave citizens risked their lives to storm the Peruvian Embassy in Havana and demand asylum. They wanted a better life—for themselves, for their families, for future generations of Cubans who would otherwise never know a world without Fidel in charge of it.

This infuriated Castro, but his narcissism wouldn't allow his reputation to be scathed. With a cigar clenched tightly in his teeth, Castro announced on a national broadcast that anyone who wanted to leave Cuba could do so, basically shouting "good riddance" as he slammed his fists on the podium, took a deep breath, and smiled.

Over the next five and a half months, close to 125,000 Cubans left their homes, their belongings, and many family members behind and poured into the United States. In a further act of evil, Fidel then opened the doors to hospitals, prisons, and asylums and sent criminals, the unwell, and sick and mentally ill people to find a new home in America. The boatlift saved many people but destroyed many more.

"Since arriving here in 1982, I have seen many men, women, and children come to freedom, Señor Pereira, and all of them are happy to be here. Why are you not smiling?"

I trusted her and reached for her hand. "I will not be free until I have my family," I said. "*Pronto sonreiré, madre.*" I'll smile soon, mother.

I will be smiling soon.

She closed her eyes and crossed herself—tracing over her forehead, lips, and heart, while whispering, "May Christ's words be on my mind, on my lips, and in my heart, and may God be with you always."

I echoed my new friend. "Always." And then, finally, a smile cracked my lips for the first time in a very long time.

Six hours later, I said goodbye to my friends. We embraced and cried, promising to always stay in touch, to always take care of each other the best we could, to always remember our journey, and to never forget what we lost.

Rafael and Javier were still trying to get in touch with relatives in Florida and Texas. Alberto would soon be met by his aunt who was driving from Tampa to take him to his new home.

And I was soon to be 30,000 feet in the air.

* * *

In Cuba, airplanes are only seen flying above the coastline. Very few planes travel cross-country. There just aren't that many places to go. Growing up, I remember watching the tiny aircraft from a distance and then hearing the roar of their engines minutes later, but I never gave them much thought.

So when I was told that I would be traveling by plane to meet my sister, I genuinely didn't know what to think. I was numb. The concept was so foreign to me, I was neither nervous nor calm.

I rode in a large white van to a gated entrance at Miami International Airport that led to the largest, most beautiful building I had ever seen. It was bright white with large glass panels, with hundreds of colorful flags flying high in front, including Cuba's. It waved proudly just below and right next to the Stars and Stripes of America. Every country in the world, it seemed, was represented, as if to say "You, yes, even you, are welcome here."

I looked out of the van window like a child arriving late to a parade. I was all but clawing at the glass, anxious to get out and excited to see what other beautiful surprises might be out there, waiting to be discovered. As the driver pulled through the security gate, I was told to gather my belongings and ready my papers so the security guard could inspect everything.

"*Buenas tardes, Señor Pereira,*" the guard greeted me. Good afternoon, Mr. Pereira. I nodded sheepishly and wondered if I was about to be arrested. "*¿Y a dónde vamos hoy?*" He continued. And where are we going today?

"*A ver a mi hermana,*" I said. To see my sister.

"Do you like country music?" he asked, still looking through my papers. When I didn't answer, he looked up at me. "*¿Te gusta la música* country? You are going to Nashville, right? Please tell me you like country music . . ."

I didn't understand what he was asking, which seemed to frustrate him, but then he continued with a smile: "Do me a favor," he said. "When you get to Nashville, tell Dolly that Robert down in Miami said hi, okay?"

I nodded my head. "*Sí, señor. Gracias.*" Yes, sir. Thank you.

"No. Thank *you*, amigo. Welcome to America." He shook his head, then shook my hand and pointed me toward a small twin-engine plane that idled about a hundred meters away.

When I sat down on the plane, an American lady who

did not speak Spanish instructed me to put my bag—my garbage bag that held all my earthly possessions—under the seat in front of me. Suddenly my nervousness became so intense, I felt like I was about to hyperventilate. I started sweating profusely and jerking my head in every direction trying to take in the sights and sounds around me: beeps and pings, the whir of the air coming from the overhead vents, the lights on the floor and above, pictures and drawings of procedures I couldn't even begin to comprehend, the roar of the engines and the spinning propellers just outside my tiny window.

I looked at the faces of the other passengers, and they looked at mine. What must they be thinking?

Why is he so scared?

Is he Cuban?

Who is this man with sunburned skin and scabs on his face?

What's in that garbage bag?

Why are his hands bandaged?

Why is he sweating so much?

Where did he get those red shoes?

None of them could possibly have imagined that just a few days ago, I was in the middle of the ocean, wondering if I would ever set foot on land again, beginning to accept my own demise.

Just then, the American lady placed her hand on my shoulder and motioned for me to fasten my seatbelt. I stared at her, confused, and my lip began to quiver.

"Shhh, it's okay. *Está bien.* You're going to be okay." And then she secured the seatbelt across my lap.

The plane jerked and began moving backward. I grabbed

the armrests of the seat and stiffened my legs to brace myself. A deep voice boomed from speakers just above my head, which made me gasp out loud.

The engines became louder and louder as the plane taxied, then stopped. Then the plane shot forward like a bullet from a gun and pressed me even deeper into my seat. My eyes were closed so tight and my grip was so strong on the armrests that I didn't even notice when the plane left the ground.

I never opened my eyes or let go of my seat. Not once throughout the entire flight. I remember being asked several questions during the two hours we were in the air, but I never answered. I never even moved.

In fact, it took three different airport personnel and a teenage girl to convince me to get off the plane after we had landed.

The girl spoke Spanish and calmly encouraged me to open my eyes.

"*Está bien. Ya está a salvo. Es hora de bajarse del avión. Lo ayudaré. Es hora de irse.*" It's okay. You're safe now. It's time to get off the plane. I will help you. It's time to go.

"*¿Estamos en Nashville?*" I asked, quietly. Are we in Nashville?

"Almost," she said. "*Ya casi ha llegado.*" You're almost there.

As we walked off the plane, she tried to prepare me for what I was about to see. "We are in Atlanta. This is the busiest airport in the world."

My knees buckled as we stepped into the terminal. Other than the facility in Miami, this was the first building I had been in since arriving in the United States. My new friend looked at me, smiling, with eyes wide, and said, "*¿Es bonito, no?*" It's pretty, isn't it?

"No," I said, with a nervous laugh.

The Atlanta airport was massive and crowded. Getting through the masses of people wasn't easy.

The girl walked with me to a wall of screens with thousands of words and flashing lights, none of which I understood or recognized. "There it is!" she exclaimed. "That's your flight. You are leaving from gate C-32. That is two terminals away. You'll have to hurry!"

She waved down a security guard who was driving a very small cart through a sea of people and explained what was happening. "He doesn't speak English," she warned, "and he has no idea where he is going."

She gave me a quick hug and told me that the officer was going to help me get to the train.

"*¿El tren?*" I asked, confused and suddenly very nervous again. The train? "*Sí.* Just go," she said. "You need to hurry!" And with that, I was whisked away through hordes of passengers in the crowded terminal. He dropped me at the top of an escalator and pointed for me to go down and get on the train. He cupped his hand in the shape of a *C* and said, "*¡Ándele, ándele!*" and motioned for me to "Go!"

I had never seen moving steps that magically appeared at one end and then disappeared at the other. It took me several attempts, but I finally clumsily landed on a single step and held on with both hands as I moved effortlessly down, down, down.

I followed the crowd to the train platform. A voice in English, then Spanish instructed me to carefully board the train and hold on. As the doors closed behind me, I felt completely alone, wondering, *What have I done? What have I done?*

The train started moving and I fell forward, crashing into a man wearing a suit and shiny leather shoes. He was none too pleased and pushed me away, mumbling something under his breath. I remember thinking that he must not be from America because he didn't look happy.

Almost as quickly as the train started moving, we began slowing down, and I grabbed the pole in front of me tightly. *"Ahora llegando a la puerta C. Puerta C . . ."* Now arriving at Gate C. Gate C. The announcement echoed throughout the car and the doors opened magically with a whoosh. The wave of people pushed by me on the platform as I stood looking at the signs and the moving stairs, now going upward to my left. The tide guided me to the steps, and I momentarily stumbled, then got both feet firmly planted. At the top, I jumped as high as I could and landed safely on solid ground.

A middle-aged woman wearing a uniform was talking with another person who looked almost as lost as I was, so I approached her calmly and handed her my ticket.

I only knew about six words in English: *Bathroom. Please. Thank you. Eat.*

And, thankfully, "Where?"

She looked at my paper. "There," she pointed to my right. Looking up, I noticed the letter *C* with numbers next to it: C-32. I made it to the gate with nineteen minutes to spare. The attendant at the gate kiosk confirmed I was, in fact, in the right place. "You will arrive in Nashville in about one hour," she said.

It had taken me almost four days to travel ninety miles in a boat. In the past four hours, I had traveled more than seven hundred miles in a van, on a plane, in a cart, and on a train. To this day, I'm not sure which journey was more tiring.

The plane to Nashville was much larger, with three seats on each side of the aisle, which made me feel safer and more secure. I wasn't nervous, and I didn't feel the stares of fellow passengers judging me. I pushed the bag under the seat in front of me, fastened my own seatbelt, opened the air vent, and breathed deeply for the first time all day.

When I closed my eyes, I saw Taire. I saw Orlando and Yusnay. I saw my father and Enier. For a few moments, I was home again, together with the people I loved, and then suddenly a forceful jerk and screeching tires pulled me back to the plane as it landed.

"Ladies and gentlemen, welcome to Nashville, where the current local time is 9:27 p.m. It is a chilly thirty-one degrees here in Music City, so bundle up, and thank you for flying with us today."

My sister, Yuny, her husband, Mikel, and about twenty strangers—friends of theirs—cheered as I walked up the Jetway into the Nashville airport. I dropped my bag and embraced Yuny. Other passengers glanced at us as they walked past, unable to understand or even acknowledge the magnitude of the moment they were witnessing. Yuny kissed me a hundred times before letting me even say hello.

"¡Estás aquí! ¡En verdad estás aquí!" You're here! You're really here!

As the others reached to pat me on the back, shake my hand, and hug my neck, I was overcome with hunger. I hadn't eaten a real meal in two days, and now relief and gratitude were replaced with the overwhelming desire to fill my stomach. Yuny promised that there was a great feast waiting for us at her home.

"*Vamos a tener una fiesta esta noche, Yosely. Es hora de celebrar.*" We're having a party tonight, Yosely. It's time to celebrate.

"Yes. Let's have a party," I said. "But first, I am going to call my wife."

13

"*ESTÁN EN CUBA*"

I HAD THE NUMBER to a community phone just a few short blocks from our house in Cumanayagua.

"*Mi corazón,*" I whispered.

I could hear Taire slide down the wall and land on the floor as she began to cry silently, desperately.

"*No digas nada, mi amor,*" I hastened. Don't say anything, my love. "*Solo escúchame.*" Just listen to me.

I knew this was not a safe phone. Government officials could definitely be listening. I spoke in abbreviations, never using our names, and never saying anything about my escape. I asked her if she was okay and told her to please kiss the children for me.

"*Tengo que irme, mi amor.*" I have to go now, my love. "*Hablaré contigo en la gasolinera.*" I'll talk to you at the gas station. "*Tengo que irme.*" I have to go.

"I love you," Taire whispered through tears. And then, click . . .

Silence.

*   *   *

For weeks, I called the gas station where Enier worked at least three times a day and never got through. It was a safer line—one the government would only attempt to bug if the financials for the station were suspicious or others from the community began to whisper.

Whenever I called, either the line was disconnected as soon as I began to speak, or the connection was never made. I became stir-crazy at my sister's apartment. I couldn't eat or sleep, and my mind was constantly racing:

What am I going to do?

How am I going to get my family out?

If I can't talk to them—if I can't get in touch with Enier—I might never see them again. I need to get a message to them. I need to talk to my wife.

I called the community phone trying to get someone, anyone, to put me in touch with Taire, but no one would allow us to talk.

Then, on my twenty-third day in America, I took more than thirty dollars in change to a pay phone next to a convenience store and finally got through.

Enier answered the phone, and when he realized it was me on the other end, he immediately became angry. "What is the matter with you? Do you know what you are doing to Taire? Do you know what you are doing to your children? What about me, *imbécil*? How dare you make promises you can't keep!" He was incensed to the point of madness until I was finally able to get a word in.

"*¡Cállate! ¡Tengo un plan, idiota!*" Shut up! I have a plan, you idiot! I screamed into the phone holding it in front of my face as if were a bullhorn. "*Escúchame.*" Listen to me.

Over the next few minutes I was able to tell Enier that I had gotten in touch with Alberto in Tampa, and we were going to find a boat—a real boat with a motor that we would use to rescue all four of them. "Tell Taire that I will call at this exact time tomorrow. Tell her that I love her, and I will see her soon."

Alberto's cousin, Chino, worked at a boatyard in Coconut Grove, near Miami. He said that we could rent a cigarette boat for seven hundred dollars if we knew how to drive it. Cigarette boats are small, fast boats that glide across the water at incredibly high speeds.

"It is a dangerous boat if you don't know how it works, but it is the best way to get in and out," he said. "It can be available in three weeks."

I certainly didn't know how to drive a boat, and I wasn't sure how I would get back to Miami. The only thing I knew for sure was that I was going to try. But first, I needed to make some money.

The next morning, before sunrise, I walked from my sister's apartment about three miles down the road to a hardware store where I was told American workers would come to pick up able-bodied men to work for cash. When I reached the pickup area, about thirty other men—all Spanish-speaking and dressed to do manual labor—were already positioned to leap into the back of pickup trucks and work vehicles. I wasn't sure what I was supposed to do, but when a second wave of 4x4s drove into the parking lot, I followed a few others and jumped in.

The driver was a middle-aged white man with a large, dark mustache. He was wearing a cowboy hat and had a huge wad of tobacco in the side of his mouth.

There were six of us in the back of his pickup, and very few words were spoken during the half-hour drive to a small construction site on a private lot of land.

The driver got out of the truck and motioned for us to get down. In broken Spanish, he tried to tell us what he needed us to do.

"*Buenos días*, gentlemen. *Mi nombre es Jim Houston.*" Good morning. My name is Jim Houston. Jim then spit out an inconceivable stream of brown saliva and extended his hand. "What's your name? I mean, *¿Cómo te llamas?*"

Taken aback by his kindness, I gingerly took his hand and said, "Yosely."

"Well, Yosely. If we're going to be friends, you're gonna have to learn how to shake hands. But that's for another day. Let's get to work, *caballeros!*" Gentlemen.

With that, he spit another line of tobacco juice and somehow explained that he needed all the construction debris next to the building cleared and put into a large dumpster located about fifteen feet away.

We worked for less than two hours and finished what Jim thought would take us all day. He was so happy and impressed that he gave us each fifty dollars and offered us sandwiches before taking us back to the hardware store parking lot. Before he drove away, he extended his hand out the truck window to me and said, "Let's see that handshake, amigo." I grabbed his hand, squeezed, and said, "*¿Mañana?*" Tomorrow?

"Yessir! I'll see you tomorrow."

On the way back to Yuny's, I stopped by the pay phone and called Taire. This was the first time we were able to actually talk with one another without fear of being over-heard, and my heart broke to hear her voice.

"How is it?" she asked. "How is America?"

It's funny. I hadn't given it much thought. Not yet, any-way. I had been so consumed with getting in touch with her to let her know that I was okay, and to try and explain why I had done what I did, that I had not yet processed where I was and what I had been doing since I arrived.

I was standing in a dirty parking lot with traffic speeding by me. To my left was a convenience store with iron bars on the windows to deter would-be thieves. To my right was a Burger King, a restaurant that served beef and french fries and something called onion rings.

Next to that was a drugstore with everything we had never been allowed to have in Cuba: more food than I had seen in my lifetime, medicine, beauty supplies, toys, books, magazines, tools, batteries, beer, soap . . . everything. Across the street, there was another drugstore, even bigger and more packed than the other. And behind me, a grocery store.

How could I even begin to describe a grocery store?

"They have different kinds of milk here," I finally said. "I haven't quite figured that out yet." We both laughed at the absurdity of it all. Hearing her voice and her beautiful laugh made me feel at home.

We talked for no more than five minutes. Taire told me that she loved me and missed me and that Orlando asked about me twenty times a day. My heart almost exploded in my chest, and I promised that I was working hard to see my family again. "It won't be long, my love. It won't be long."

"*Ten cuidado, Yosely*," she begged.
Be careful.

*　*　*

A few weeks later, I spoke to Enier. He said that Taire was starting to get a lot of attention from neighbors and the policia. "When Taire arrived home from the gas station the last time I talked with her, Luisa was waiting on the front steps of your house.

"'Where have you been, Taire?' Luisa asked, as if she was already accusing Taire of a crime." Enier explained that Taire didn't get angry, but she did have a quick and elevated response to Luisa. "How many times do I need to tell you, Luisa? My business is my business. When have I ever asked you about your life?" I imagined the scowl on Taire's face as Enier continued.

"Never," Taire said, taking a step closer to Luisa and facing off to confront her. "But I have nothing to hide . . . Do you?"

Enier was laughing as he recounted the confrontation to me.

"Yosely, Taire was just a few inches from Luisa's face and growled, 'I have a lot of secrets, and if you are not careful, you will find out more than you want to know.'"

He said Luisa turned and started toward her front door and then stepped back and straightened her shoulders.

"Where is your husband, Taire?" Luisa demanded. "Why did he leave you?"

Enier was enjoying telling me the story. "Whipping around, Taire made a beeline straight to our curious friend and smiled. 'Maybe he didn't leave me, Luisa. Have you ever let yourself think of that? Maybe he's just gone. Would you like to know where I buried his body?'

"Can't you just imagine the look on Luisa's face, Yosely?" Enier was laughing at the thought. "She was so stunned by Taire's reply, she almost fell backward into her miserable house."

Enier and I laughed for a few moments, both marveling at Taire's grit. Then Enier's voice softened. "She can't stay this strong forever, Yosely. You need to think of something. Soon."

With that, he hung up the phone and left me to ponder my wife's strength and courage. It would be many weeks before I could tell her myself.

Many miserable weeks.

* * *

In the meantime, I met Jim at the hardware store every morning, and he would take a group of us to different sites where we would move debris and clean up construction projects.

Jim was a retired architect who still kept busy designing various buildings and homes throughout the state. He acted as a sort of foreman after his designs were finalized and the projects were underway. He was always very kind and seemed to take a special interest in me—even inviting me to ride with him in the cab of his truck from time to time.

I worked very hard for Jim, and it wasn't lost on him that I took very few water breaks and worked through lunch. I knew the harder I worked and the more projects I could complete, the more money I could send to Chino in Miami.

One evening as we were driving back to the hardware store, Jim began asking me a lot of questions. I understood very little of what he said, but occasionally I would try to engage.

"*Su familia,*" he said. Your family. "*¿Tiene familia?*" Do you have a family?

"*Sí.* I have family," I said.

"Is that why you work so hard? *¿Trabajo?* For your family?"

"*Sí.* Yes."

"Where are they?" he asked, straining his neck to try and make eye contact. "Are they here? In the United States?"

I looked up from my gaze on the dashboard and met his eyes.

"No, sir." I cleared my throat. "*Están en Cuba.*" They're in Cuba.

Jim exhaled as if he had just been punched in the gut. "Cuba," he repeated. "I've never met anyone from Cuba before . . ."

We were both silent for the rest of the trip home. When we pulled into the parking lot of the hardware store, Jim finally spoke up. "I'll pray for your family, Yosely. And I'll see you in the morning." With that, he handed me a hundred-dollar bill and nodded. "I'll see you tomorrow."

I now had nine hundred dollars, so I called Alberto to tell him I would see him soon. I dared not tell Yuny my plan to rent a boat, but I did tell her that I wanted to visit my friends in Miami.

The next morning, I didn't meet Jim in the parking lot; instead, Yuny dropped me at a bus station in downtown Nashville, where I bought a one-way ticket for $114 and began a twenty-four-hour journey to meet Chino in Coconut Grove.

* * *

JUNE 2002

Just before lunchtime the next day, I arrived in Florida, where Alberto was waiting at the bus station. I couldn't miss him in his bright yellow sweatsuit with white stripes along the sleeves and legs, and braided leather shoes the color of the inside of an orange peel. When I stepped down from the bus steps, he removed his enormous sunglasses and rushed to give me a hug.

"Yosely! Hermano! You look awful! What are they doing to you in Tennessee?"

I was exhausted. I didn't even have the energy to make fun of his shoes. And those glasses? I couldn't imagine what he had done—or what had been done to him—that made him agree to look so ridiculous.

After we hugged and he made a few more comments about what I was wearing—jeans, a short-sleeved button-down shirt, and my red Nikes—he escorted me to a car that was waiting behind the bus station.

"*Este es mi primo, Chino,*" he said. This is my cousin, Chino. "He will show you the boat. Do you have the money?"

I pulled a handkerchief from my back pocket, unwrapped it, and counted out the money: $723.00.

"Is that all of your money?" Alberto asked. "How are you going to get back to Tennessee?"

I wasn't concerned with getting back to Nashville. My family was ninety miles away, and that is all that mattered. Alberto shook his head and told us that he would meet Chino and me the next afternoon to discuss the plan. He said he had some business to take care of in Fort Lauderdale.

"What kind of business?" I asked.

"First of all, I am going to find you a new pair of shoes," he joked, "but then, it's my business. You just go with Chino. He'll take good care of you. *Te veré mañana.*" I'll see you tomorrow.

I got in the car and Chino drove for about twenty minutes, heading southwest toward the boatyard. We didn't say much to each other. I was too focused on what was going to happen the next day, and I don't think Chino wanted a lot of information. He had his money.

"There she is." He slowed the car and pointed to a speedboat anchored to the docks between two large fishing boats. "The owners trust me. I keep it very clean. Are you sure you know how to drive it?"

"*Por supuesto.*" Of course.

I lied. But how difficult could it be? I had driven manual transmissions before, and this didn't even have a clutch. I had captained a twelve-foot wooden boat through the Florida Straits. I felt certain I could push a lever and skid across ninety miles of waves in a boat that could exceed speeds of ninety miles per hour.

"Well, the weather looks good tomorrow night. You

shouldn't have any problems." Chino turned and looked at me as he pulled a cigarette from his shirt pocket and lit it. After a long drag, he exhaled and said, "She must be pretty special. Your wife, I mean. Alberto told me what you did to get here. Are you sure you want to go back?"

A lump formed in my throat, and I looked him dead in the eye. "Nothing will keep me from my family," I said.

"*Te creo, hermano.*" I believe you, brother. Chino took another quick inhale of his cigarette and flicked it out of the window.

"*Comamos.*" Let's eat.

We went to Chino's apartment where his girlfriend made us *ropa vieja*, a classic Cuban meal of shredded beef stewed in fresh tomatoes, onions, peppers, garlic, and wine. She had also prepared white rice, black beans, and sweet plantains, but I couldn't eat anything. Nerves had my stomach in knots, especially since I hadn't been able to get in touch with Enier about where exactly to meet me.

Ever since I learned that Chino could secure a boat, I had been researching potential extraction points for my family. I had asked Enier to scout the locations in the evenings. He had visited four places over the past two weeks, but only one—Matanzas—had deep enough water on the coastline to allow everyone to jump in the water and swim to meet the boat.

We agreed on a plan: Enier would take Taire and the kids on a trip through Santa Clara to Matanzas the next day. There was an electrical facility with large smokestacks near that point that could be seen from a distance in the ocean. This would serve as the focal point for where I would meet them. But Enier and I had never discussed a specific time.

It was late, but I tried calling the gas station one more time. I was shocked when Enier answered. "Yosely," he whispered. "We have a problem. Taire is being followed. They have even followed her here. I don't know how we can get to the coast."

Luisa had alerted the policia that Taire was up to something, and they had been following her for several days. Two armed officers were on her tail everywhere she turned. On the road to her parents' house, they were behind her. At the ration station where she picked up food and milk, they were there. Three days in a row, she had tried to meet Enier at the gas station, and they were there, waiting. They had even picked up Enier and questioned him the night before as he made his way back to Cienfuegos from Matanzas.

"Yosely, we are trapped. I don't know how to . . ."

I interrupted him midsentence. "You have to try! Enier, listen to me," I pleaded. "I have a boat. I am leaving tomorrow after dark, and I will meet you at the shore. Promise me you will try."

My heart sank into my stomach and I began to weep. "Enier, I am coming for you," I said. "Please. Please be there."

Enier paused and then said, "Okay, hermano, okay. We will try."

That night, I prayed that God would protect my family. "No matter what happens to me," I begged, "please just keep them safe."

The next morning, Alberto arrived at Chino's apartment just before ten. We sat and watched TV for several hours. He and Chino drank beer and tried to talk me out of going back to Cuba.

"There is nothing on this earth that could make me go back there," Alberto said. His voice cracked as he continued, "She is lucky to have you, Yosely."

"No," I said, standing, ready to leave. "I am lucky to have her. The sun will be setting soon. It's time to go."

Alberto and Chino looked at each other, gulped down the last of their beers, and got up. "*Vámonos.*"

At the docks, Alberto and Chino quickly untied the boat, and Alberto kissed me on each cheek before pushing me out into the waterway with his foot. "We'll see you in a few hours, Yosely! We'll be here waiting for you!"

Suddenly, I was moving farther and farther away, and then it hit me. *I don't know how to start the engine!* I looked around frantically for the key, but there wasn't one. Just a red button next to the throttle.

"God be with me," I said, as I looked to the night sky and pushed the button.

The sound of a powerboat's engine is deafening, like a hundred motorcycles being revved at the same time. As the roar continued, I almost panicked, but then reached under the steering wheel and found a switch that turned on the internal lights of the boat.

The dashboard panel lit up showing a compass that was pointing northwest. *I need to be going the other way!* I thought, and then pushed ever so slightly on the throttle.

The boat jumped out from under me and pressed me into the seat, where I was able to regain my composure and straighten the nose of the boat toward the open water. I pushed the throttle a bit more and began skimming at a pace faster than I was comfortable with—thirty kilometers per hour. At this rate, I would never make it back to the docks before daylight.

Once I reached open water, I was able to position the boat south by southwest, with the compass pointing in the exact longitude and latitude coordinates on Chino's map.

I started pushing the boat faster and faster, unable to see more than three feet in front of the boat but trusting the sea to be as desolate and free from obstruction as it was a few weeks earlier when I passed over this same water in the opposite direction.

I started having flashbacks of that journey. The desperation, pain, hunger, and thirst we experienced welled up an indescribable sadness in me. It was more than my mind could hold. But here I was again, anticipating a joyful reunion with my Taire, my North Star.

An uncontrollable scream erupted from my chest and I stood up, directly facing the wind and water, and pressed even harder on the throttle. Fifty kilometers per hour; sixty; seventy; eighty. The sea was like glass, without a wave in sight. Without another boat or flashing light from land to be seen.

This was really happening. I was going to make it. I prayed out loud for the first time since I had been in these waters:

"Dios mío, por favor, quédate conmigo. Me lo prometiste. Por favor, protege a mi familia . . ." Dear God, please stay with

me. You promised. Please protect my family." With that, I screamed, "Amen!" and pressed forward even faster.

Almost three hours after leaving the dock in Coconut Bay, I began to see indistinguishable formations ahead. The moon was hidden by large clouds directly above me, and I couldn't tell what was there. I knew I had to be getting close to the island, so I pulled back on the throttle to a trolling speed for the rest of the way.

Even though there were still no lights on shore, as far as I could tell I had picked a good place to meet Taire and Enier. There was no policia or coast guard patrolling this particular spot.

Then, forms began to take shape and I saw plumes of smoke rising in the distance. I could see the tops of palm trees and the shapes of large buildings. The compass had me pointed exactly toward my mark, so I pressed the red button to stall the engines. I would coast from here.

For the next hour and a half, I floated almost completely still and watched the shore for a sign—any sign—that Enier had gotten Taire and the kids safely out of Cumanayagua. A flash of light. A sound. Anything. But there was nothing. They weren't there.

They weren't coming.

Just then, I heard a boat motor on my left, getting louder and louder. It could only be one thing—the police were coming. They had heard me or seen me or someone else had heard or seen me and reported the cigarette boat.

There was nothing I could do. Nowhere for me to hide.

I pushed the red button again and screamed as the engines roared. I had to turn around and go back. Alone.

The return trip was much faster. I can't recall a single thought that went through my head. I don't remember ever looking down at the compass. I just sped forward and then found myself being greeted by Alberto and Chino. They had fallen asleep on the dock surrounded by empty beer bottles, and the sound of the cigarette boat woke them up.

Chino jumped into the water and swam to meet me and help guide the boat to its slip.

Alberto raised his hands outward, "*¿Qué pasó?*" What happened?

I pulled myself onto the dock and pushed past my friend. "They weren't there," I said.

"*¿Y ahora?*" What happens now? he asked, hurriedly picking up the bottles and starting after me. "Yosely! What are you going to do?"

"It was stupid for me to ask them to do something so dangerous. I don't know what I was thinking. It's too dangerous, too dangerous." I kept repeating over and over.

"I have to make some more money," I called back. "We have to find another way."

The next morning, I was on another Greyhound bus heading north to Nashville. Chino felt bad for me and paid for my ticket.

Thirty-six hours after leaving the coast of Cuba without my family, I was standing in the hardware store parking lot in East Nashville waiting for Jim.

14

ALL THE HELP I CAN GET

THE SMILE ON Jim's face when he saw me waiting in the parking lot was like a child's after receiving a gift. He waved and rolled down the passenger window of his truck. "Hey there, Cuba! Where have you been, amigo? Hop in, we've got a lot of work to do."

I was so tired. The past three days had taken a toll, and I fell asleep in the truck almost immediately. When we stopped, Jim shook me awake. We were sitting in the driveway of a house that looked like a castle to me.

"Welcome to my home," Jim said. "C'mon, let me show you around."

The grounds were immaculate. The grass looked like green velvet, stretched from end to end with perfectly placed islands of pine straw and an array of bright red, pink, yellow, and white flowers. The house was whitewashed brick with black shutters and a bright red front door.

In the backyard was a swimming pool in the shape of a kidney bean, surrounded by so many flowers and such lush greenery that it made the national botanical gardens in Havana look malnourished and sad. The yard blended seamlessly into a tree-shaded cove connected to a dark blue and green lake as still as glass.

This was the most peaceful place I had ever been.

By the time I got my wits about me, I saw the other four workers moving shovelfuls of red dirt and mulch and pallets of fresh lumber from the platform of a flatbed truck to an unfinished area of the property behind a stretch of trees.

"*Ven aquí.*" Come here. Jim was standing next to a shed near the lake's edge, calling and waving me over. I quickly joined him, wiping the sleep from my eyes.

"*Lo siento, señor.*" I'm sorry, sir.

"There's no need to apologize, amigo. But if you feel up to it, I sure could use your help in here."

Jim opened the door to the shed to reveal a workshop full of tools. Carpentry tools! The walls were lined with brand-new hammers, measures, levels, knives, squares, handsaws, and chisels. A circular saw, a reciprocating saw, a miter saw, compressors, drills, and enough nails and screws to build an entire city were arranged on workbenches and shelves.

Jim could see the amazement on my face. "Do you know how to use any of this stuff?" he asked, pointing at a saw. He held his arms up as if to say, "I certainly don't."

I could tell what he was asking, and I quickly said, "*¡Sí! Soy carpintero.*" I'm a carpenter.

"*Carpintero.*" He repeated. "You're a carpenter?"

"*¡Sí!*" I shouted. "*En Cuba, era carpintero.*" In Cuba, I was a carpenter.

"Well, why didn't you say so?" Jim patted me on the back

and started laughing. "I knew I liked you, amigo. Come here and take a look at this!"

He showed me sketches and blueprints for a small building. "My wife is an artist and I want to build her a studio where she can paint, draw, work with clay, or simply get away." Jim's drawings were beautiful, but he needed help bringing it to life.

I looked over the drawings carefully for several minutes and glanced up to see Jim studying me just as closely. I put my finger to my chest and said, "*Lo puedo construir.*" I can build this.

And that's what I did. Every day for a month, I worked late into the evening, stopping occasionally only to eat or to try to contact Enier at the gas station. We would talk every few days, and I would send messages to Taire and Orlando through him.

"Tell Orlando that I am with him, always. Tell Taire that I still do not like mangoes. Make sure you tell them that I love them. I will see you all soon, hermano. *Lo prometo.*" I promise.

I was also in almost daily contact with Alberto. He said he knew people who might be able to help rescue Taire and the others. "When can you come back to Miami and meet them?" he kept asking, over and over again.

"When I have money. I will come when I have money."

I missed my family, and each sunset seemed to take them further and further away.

I thought of Taire being watched, questioned, or criticized. When she was lying in bed, feeling government agents outside her window. Waking up and seeing them standing in front of the house, smoking in the empty street. Catching them sneakily peering over their sunglasses or stoically staring, arms crossed, like bodyguards.

How long could she take it? How many more days would she have to respond to questions for which everyone already knew the answers?

It was widely known that I had escaped to America. And there were very few questions about who went with me.

Everyone already knew.

When five men go missing on the same night, they have either been taken to prison, escaped, or died trying.

What more were they hoping to learn from her and Enier? What crime were they guilty of?

How much longer would she have to be afraid to go outside or allow the kids to play in the yard? How many more knocks at the door would there be as curious officials leaned inside to intimidate and pressure Taire for information?

* * *

I spoke to Enier two weeks after the failed rescue plan and learned what had happened that night. Enier had been stopped by the police and was arrested for failing to produce the appropriate paperwork for the vehicle he was driving. He was taken to Cienfuegos and held for four days. Meanwhile, Taire had no idea what had happened and feared the worst. When Enier returned to Cumanayagua four days later, he had two broken ribs and close to three hundred stitches in the back of his head.

Taire invited him to stay with her and the kids for a few weeks while he recovered. They were already being watched and rumors were rampant throughout the entire region about her relationship with my best friend, so what difference could it make?

To make matters worse, the water was disconnected, and Taire was told that their rations were being decreased because I was no longer there.

They were prisoners.

That's why the policia were following her, to remind her that she wasn't going anywhere. None of them were. Even thinking otherwise was a crime punishable by harassment, beatings, and withholding of basic human rights—especially food and water.

*   *   *

My days were full, and they passed very quickly. Jim dropped me at his house every morning after taking a crew to one or more of his worksites.

Most days, I worked alone, but sometimes he would sit with me, offer to help, or ask me questions about carpentry, Cuba, or my family. Oftentimes he would take an opportunity to teach me English, motioning to the sky: *That is a bird.* Holding a hammer: *Ham-err.* Or pointing to various parts of his body: *Hair. Eyes. Teeth. Hand. Shoe.*

One late afternoon, as I was very close to finishing the studio, Jim brought his wife, Linda, to meet me and see the progress we had made. She was overwhelmed and impressed with my work, admiring the cabinetry, shelves, and extra design details I had put in the backsplash behind her new sink. Then she stretched out her arms with a huge smile and gave me a hug.

"Oh, Yosely, it's beautiful! *¡Qué bonito!*" Looking around the room, she covered her mouth and continued, "Jim, it's perfect. It is just wonderful. Thank you."

"Don't thank me," he said, blushing. "This is all Yosely. He is a true genius."

Linda looked at Jim and whispered something to him. He nodded. "Of course! Yes."

Looking at me, Jim then said, "*Mi esposa* . . . my wife . . . she would like to . . . um, *quiere invitarte* . . . uh, she would like to invite you to dinner . . . *a cenar. ¿Está bien?*"

I nodded yes and followed the two of them into their home. After washing my hands, I joined them in the kitchen. Jim handed me a beer and told me to sit. "The steaks will be done in just a few minutes," he said. "You do like steak, right? *¿Te gusta la carne?*"

I nodded emphatically. "Yes! It's good!"

Truth is, I couldn't remember ever having a steak. Beef is illegal in Cuba. The few times I had eaten beef back home were certainly nothing like this.

As Jim returned outside to tend the grill, Linda kept bringing different dishes to the table: various chips and dips and salsa; grilled corn; watermelon, strawberries, and grapes; baked potatoes; salad with cucumber, tomatoes, and cheese.

"Tell me about your family," Linda said, smiling, and looking over her shoulder from the kitchen sink. "Jim tells me you have two young children?"

I nodded. "Yes, ma'am," I said, softly, trying not to make eye contact.

"I bet they are wonderful! Tell me all about them!" Linda's smile was beautiful and warm. Kindness radiated from her eyes as she listened so intently to every detail about Orlando and Yusnay.

When Jim finally came back into the kitchen, he was carrying a tray of steaks. He put the platter in front of me and slapped me on the back.

"I hope you're hungry," he said.

Linda grabbed my hands and gave them a slight squeeze. "I can't wait to meet them," she said with a wink. "All three of them."

As we began to eat, Jim and Linda explained that they had wanted to have kids but they had never been able to. "I guess the good Lord had other plans," Jim said with a smile. "I guess He knew that this gal . . ." he patted Linda's knee under the table, "I guess He knew she would be all I ever needed to keep my heart full."

I could see their love for each other was deep. There was a tenderness to both of them that only love could create. It made me miss my Taire even more.

I was suddenly overcome with emotion and ran onto the deck behind the house. I heard the door open, and Jim slowly approached as I began to weep.

I was thinking about Taire. My kids. My friends. My family. *What are they eating tonight? A piece of bread? Rice again? Beans? Does Yusnay have enough formula? Where are they? What are they doing? I should never have left them. What have I done?*

For the next two hours, I bared my soul to Jim. The language barrier made it difficult, but he listened and tried to comfort me as best he could. He hurt for me and with me. I knew that he understood.

"How can I help you, Yosely? How can I help your family?"

After a few deep breaths, I looked at Jim and said, very plainly, in English: "I need money. I need to go to Miami."

* * *

OCTOBER 2002

Two days later, I was in Miami again after another grueling bus ride from Nashville. Jim purchased a round-trip ticket and paid me $2,000 for my work on Linda's studio. Alberto picked me up at the bus station very early in the morning. He was going to introduce me to his boss, Rúben, at dinner.

Rúben was a lawyer in Miami, whose parents were Cuban. I didn't understand what Alberto did in Rúben's organization. When I asked him, he simply said, "I just run errands and make deliveries from time to time. It's very good money."

But Alberto was certain Rúben could help me. "He has a lot of connections, and I have told him all about you."

Alberto took me to Chino's apartment, where I slept for several hours. When I woke up, I took a shower and was surprised when Alberto laid a pair of tan dress pants and a blue silk shirt on the bed. "I brought you some clothes. You cannot go to dinner dressed as a Cuban carpenter."

"But I *am* a Cuban carpenter."

"Not today, hermano," he said, smiling. "Today, you are a businessman. Do you have the money?"

I assured my friend that I had plenty of cash and began to put on the ridiculous outfit he insisted I wear.

We arrived at the Forge restaurant in Miami Beach just before six o'clock. Alberto pulled up to the valet and shouted through the passenger side window, "I'm just making a delivery!" and shooed the uniformed driver away.

"You're not coming in?" I asked, surprised and suddenly more nervous than I had been in a long time.

"*No, amigo. ¡Es muy caro!*" No, friend. It's very expensive! Winking and then reaching across my waist to unlatch the door, he smiled, "I hope you brought your wallet."

Alberto had given me a description of Rúben: a short, plump man in his fifties with slicked-back gray hair, who wore jeweled rings on almost every finger. "You can't miss him," he said. "He will be the one who looks like he belongs in there."

The Forge is a vast and ornate museum-like restaurant with rich, mahogany-covered walls and chandeliers that sparkle like a thousand diamonds overhead. It only took a few moments to spot Rúben, sitting in the back of the restaurant.

My arms and legs started getting weak as I made my way to his table. Rúben looked up and motioned for me to sit.

I swallowed hard and began to speak: "*Me llamo Yosely Pereira. Soy amigo de Alberto . . .*" My name is Yosely Pereira. I'm Alberto's friend . . .

"In English! Please!" Rúben demanded. "You are in America now!"

I was taken aback by his gravelly voice and froze, terrified, like a beaten puppy.

"I'm sorry. I didn't mean to startle you," he said. "But I think it would be best if we communicate in my language, if it's all the same to you."

I understood just a few words he said, but I nodded.

"Are you eating? Best food in Miami, bar none."

"No, thank you," I said as clearly as I could.

"Your loss, amigo," Rúben grunted, placing another huge piece of meat in his mouth. "So, why are you here? My new employee tells me you have a proposition for me."

I didn't understand the question. I simply responded with, "My family."

Taking a large gulp of wine, Rúben nodded, "Yes, your family. They are in Cuba, no?"

"Yes, I need my family."

"Take it easy, friend. I understand." Leaning toward me, Rúben motioned for me to come closer too.

"I know people," he whispered. "I can help you."

"Oh, gracias," I yelled, then quickly placed both hands over my mouth. "Gracias. I have money."

Rúben's eyes widened, sparked with fury. "Shut up, you fool! I thought you were a businessman!"

"I am. I mean, what do I need to do?"

"You need to calm down," Rúben quietly demanded. "I have friends with a boat . . ."

"No boats," I interrupted him. "I cannot put my family on a boat."

"I understand. It's okay. This is not like the boat you paddled here in, I promise. It's a big boat."

"No," I said again. "I will not put my family on a boat."

Rúben placed his hands behind his neck, exhaled, and nodded.

"Okay. No boats."

He paused for a moment, then leaned forward, never taking his eyes off mine.

Finally, he blinked.

"How do you feel about marriage?"

15

HOW DO YOU FEEL ABOUT MARRIAGE?

WEEKS PASSED. I knew that Taire was growing more and more anxious each day. Whenever we talked, her voice sounded different. She said that she would do anything to have our family whole again, but there was no conviction in her voice. The constant cycle of longing and wondering without any resolution had extinguished her small flame of hope.

I talked with Enier every now and then, but it was too dangerous for me to speak at length with Taire. She and Enier decided to stop seeing each other as often, but Enier promised he would come to her immediately if he heard from me.

I managed to get a few messages through Enier to Taire:

Tell Taire to trust me.

Tell her I love her.

Tell Orlando I am with him, always.

Enier was getting frustrated too. "Your updates are beginning to feel like sharp daggers, reminding me that you are free and we are not. Taire has never stopped loving you." Enier's voice began to crack. "She misses you more every single day, but how much longer do you think she's going to believe that you're going to rescue her? This is beginning to be cruel, Yosely. This time, your plan has to work!"

When I called Enier with my new plan, I asked him to explain it to Taire. I knew better than to tell Taire myself— not for fear of being caught, but for fear of her reaction.

He told me later that when he relayed my plan to Taire, "her mouth was gaping like a sinkhole, and her eyes were the size of cantaloupes. I tried to calm her down, Yosely," he sputtered, but she was "*muy, muy enojada*." Very, very angry. "She started breaking things in the house, hermano!"

He pleaded with her, "Taire, you must keep your voice down. Let me explain."

The next few hours must have been hell for my friend. How was he to explain to my wife that her husband— the man who had deserted his family and friends months ago, the same man who had promised he would always be with her and always love her—now wanted her to marry someone else?

Enier locked the door and ushered her into the kitchen in the middle of the house. "Por favor, Taire," he whispered and put his arms around her.

"Yosely's plan will work," he said. "You have to trust me. You have to trust him. He will always be your husband. And he will always be my brother. We just have to trust him."

*   *   *

Rúben had a business associate in Mexico named Marco, who traveled regularly to Havana. Mexico was the only Latin American country that had maintained diplomatic ties with

Cuba throughout the Cold War, even after Fidel had angered the Mexican government by making disparaging remarks about its people.

That incident led the Mexican ambassador to leave Havana, but business was business. As long as Mexico helped line Fidel's pockets through trade and investments, he allowed businessmen to travel back and forth between the two countries.

For a fee, Marco agreed to marry Taire in Havana, allowing her to become a naturalized Mexican citizen. That would give Taire the opportunity to more easily escape to the United States.

I hated the idea of Taire pledging her love to another man—even if it was not sincere. We had committed ourselves to one another when we were married. She had my whole heart and I had hers. But that's why we had to try. That's why this hoax had to work.

"God, forgive me. We have to try."

It sounded like a far-fetched plan to me, but Rúben said he had seen it work in the past. "This will not be easy," he said, "especially with the children. But Marco will do it. He will try."

"And what about my friend? What about Enier?"

"It will take a few weeks, but he will be able to visit his 'sister' in Mexico after she is settled. You will just need $5,000."

Just $5,000?

Where in the world am I going to get $5,000?

I called Jim from the pay phone across the street from Yuny's apartment and tried to explain what was happening. "You don't owe me an explanation, my friend," he said.

"Linda and I would be honored to help you." His words brought a lump to my throat, and I couldn't find the words to tell him how much I appreciated him. "Gracias, hermano." Thank you, my brother, was all I could muster.

I borrowed $3,000 from Jim and combined the loan with everything I had saved to that point. I had a total of $5,200.

Jim wired the money to Rúben in Miami, and I went back to Tennessee to work on the art studio.

* * *

MARCH 2003

The day my family was ready to leave for Havana, I had second thoughts. *What if the plan doesn't work? What if it does work and Taire would rather stay in Mexico with Marco? What if they are arrested trying to leave the country?*

I came to work but I was consumed with anxiety and unable to focus.

Jim met me inside the studio with a glass of lemonade. "Let's not work today," he said. "I think we should sit by the lake, look at the water, and talk. What do you think?"

And that's what we did for the entire afternoon. I told Jim how Taire and I met. He laughed and laughed at the story of my missing shoe from the day of her uncle's funeral. I told Jim how my father had taught me carpentry. When I described the beauty of my country, he closed his eyes and tried to imagine it.

For that time, on that day, we were two friends simply enjoying each other's company. Even more than the money he loaned me, that was the greatest gift Jim ever gave me. I don't think I could have endured that day alone.

That night, I imagined my family walking slowly into a barrio crowded with buildings.

I imagined Taire peeking into a once-grand entryway, now draped in poverty, then pushing the children to climb a ramshackle staircase leading to what seemed like nothing at all.

Could this really be the way to freedom?

I imagined her being met at the top of the stairs by a well-dressed, very handsome man who introduced himself as Marco Ramirez. "Hola, señora. I am a business associate of your husband's," he said with a smile.

Looking at the children, he cocked his head and took a deep breath. "Hola, niños."

Taire would fall in love with him.

Oh, God! How could I have allowed this to happen? I'll never see them again!

My thoughts were interrupted by the phone ringing. It was Enier, calling me from a nearby hotel. "Yosely, I have the children. We are safe."

"And Taire? How is she?"

"She is fine. She is . . ." He paused. "She is with her fiancé."

"You left them alone!" I was furious and sick to my stomach.

"It's okay, hermano. He is okay."

He then told me that Taire's anger toward me and her nervousness about the situation subsided after meeting Marco. She became excited about the possibility of the plan working. "Marco is very nice, and he truly wants to help you and your family."

"Can I speak to Orlando?"

Enier suddenly whispered, "Sorry. I have to go. We'll talk again soon."

I could only imagine what was happening in Havana. A lot had to be done in order to pull this off.

They need to secure papers.

They need a cake.

They need rings.

Photos need to be taken.

What about the children?

Everything had already been paid for, but they would need to stay very busy if the wedding was going to happen before Marco and my family left for Mexico in two days.

I couldn't sleep, thinking about what was going to take place the next morning.

Taire will be dressed in the same gown she wore for me in La Perla del Sur. She will be breathtaking.

I envisioned Enier and the kids walking with her to the park to meet Marco. *He will be dressed perfectly for the wedding. They will look happy, the perfect couple.*

Enier will photograph them in the park. Taire, holding flowers, will pretend to laugh and smile and make the most of a very bizarre afternoon. Five-year-old Orlando will be so confused.

He'll ask a lot of questions, and everyone will convince him that they are just playing a game.

I didn't have to imagine the next part. Rúben had filled me in on the details.

"After the photographs are taken, they will make their way to the government office where marriage licenses are distributed. They will pay thirty Cuban pesos, and then they will be legally married. Then, her name will be officially recorded as Taire Ramirez. It's as simple as that . . . but the visas will be a bit more difficult."

"What do you mean?" I asked.

"They will have to prove their love. They will have to convince the registrar that their relationship is true." Then he added, "I hope they study."

"Study? For what?" I said, starting to panic.

In my mind, I could see Taire and her new husband walking with the children to an office building next door, guarded by a twenty-foot statue of an angry Fidel shaking his fist at passersby.

"For the questions that the registrar will ask," Rúben said. Then he went through the list as if Taire were standing in front of him.

Where did you meet?

Havana.

How long have you known each other?

Almost a year.

Have you been married before?

Yes.

How many times?

Once.

What happened to your first husband?

He left.

He left?

Yes. I haven't seen him in a very long time.

Interesting. Where will you live?

Mexico.

Why?

My husband's business is there.

Do you have family in Cuba?

Yes.

Where do they live?

Lomitas, Cumanayagua.

"They will then sit in that room and be told to look straight ahead, silently, until the registrar returns. After she reviews the paperwork, the attendant will return with the visas and everything will be okay," Rúben said.

Enier called me again from the hotel lobby.

"Something must be wrong, Yosely. They've been in there for hours!"

"In where? What is happening, Enier?"

"The wedding was a success. It was quite beautiful, really. You should have been there."

"I'm not in the mood for jokes, Enier. What's happening?"

"Taire and Marco have been inside with the visa officers for three hours. I'm afraid something is wrong."

With that, the line went dead. I sat at the end of my bed in silence, unable to even picture my beloved.

* * *

I didn't hear anything for several days. Then when I was finishing up some site work with Jim and his crew, Rúben called.

"Yosely. Amigo," he greeted me. "I have a bit of bad news. It's not the end of the world, but the whole marriage thing didn't work out. I know you are probably more than a little bit disappointed, but, hey, I told you it wasn't going to be easy. Listen, I still have options for you, and I will discuss them with you just as soon as I get back from a business trip to Colorado. I'll give you a call, okay, amigo? Yosely, are you there?"

He was speaking so fast in English, I hardly understood a word. All I knew was my wife and children were still in Cuba.

"Yosely? Did I lose you?" Rúben said.

"I'm here." I managed to push the words out slowly.

"So, yeah, I'm sorry that deal didn't work for you, but I promise I'll call you soon." With that, our conversation ended.

I had been standing there in silence for several minutes looking at my phone when Jim came up to me. My expression told him everything.

"It didn't work?" he asked.

I shook my head slowly from side to side and then my body went limp. Jim caught and held me until I could collect myself. "Let's get you home."

Jim drove me to Yuny's apartment and told me not to worry about working the rest of the week. When I said I needed the hours to make money, he stopped me. "That is the least of your concerns right now. We will work all that out just as soon as you rest and we figure out what to do next. Okay?"

"Thank you, Jim," I said, getting out of the truck and heading to the apartment door.

"Yosely," he called out, "we're going to get your family to America, do you understand? Don't give up on me. Don't give up on them either. It's gonna happen."

Looking back, Jim's kindness and encouraging words were exactly what I needed in those excruciating moments, but I couldn't accept them yet. I wasn't ready for more promises. I wasn't prepared to have hope. That night, I tossed and turned and barely slept.

What had Rúben meant when he said, "I still have options"? What else can we possibly do?

I slept past ten the next morning and woke to a dead battery on my phone. No one else was in the apartment, and I couldn't find a charger. I needed to call Enier. I had to talk with Taire. My mind was racing, and I felt like I would go crazy if I didn't get in touch with them right then. I rushed to the convenience store with a ten-dollar bill and asked the clerk for quarters. He only had enough change for five dollars, but it was enough to at least call the gas station in Cumanayagua.

I shakily put the quarters one by one in the slot and dialed the number. As the phone began to ring, I thought I might hyperventilate until, finally . . .

"Hola." It was Enier.

"Hermano! Oh, Enier, it is good to hear your voice. How is Taire?"

"Hola," he said again.

"Enier, are you okay? Is Taire okay?" I pleaded for him to answer.

"*Pregúntale,*" he said, sounding depressed and tired. "Ask her yourself. She's right here."

My heart sank and I almost dropped the phone receiver.

"Taire! My love. My heart. How are you?"

"Yosely?" She said my name as if she didn't believe it was me. "Oh, Yosely." She started crying, and every emotion I had experienced over the past few months came rushing to the surface. I slid down the wall of the phone booth and wept with her.

"Yosely, I don't have much time. I have to go back to work. I love you, my husband. I love you, my heart. I have to go now. They will get suspicious. Call back soon, okay?"

"No! Wait! Don't leave!" I screamed through the phone, but my time was up, and I was left with a click and the deafening buzz of a dial tone.

I ran as quickly as I could to the drugstore on the opposite street corner to try and exchange my other five dollars, but they wouldn't do it. I tried the Burger King, and they also declined. At the grocery store, the clerk said that I needed to buy something before she could give me change, so I grabbed a pack of pink bubblegum and handed her my money.

Running back to the pay phone, I counted three dollars and seventy-six cents, which was barely enough to even get through. Again, I put the money in the slot as if my life depended on it and dialed the number very carefully.

Enier answered again.

"You can't keep calling, Yosely," he said before I could even say hello. "It's killing her."

"Enier, please. What was Taire talking about? What work did she need to get back to? What's going on?"

"The officials from the school came to the house a few days ago," he said. "They do not have enough teachers, and she has no way to buy food, so . . ."

"So she is back working for the government?" I asked, surprised and somehow hurt by what he was saying.

"See, that's just it," he shot back. "She's not working for the government. She's working for her family. She's doing what she has to do. Her husband left her, you know?"

As soon as those words left his mouth the phone went dead again. I don't know how long I stood motionless in that phone booth, but for several minutes the world went almost completely dark and all sound disappeared. Surely this was all a dream—a quiet nightmare that still held Taire prisoner. A nightmare in which my best friend resented me. One that allowed my children to grow up without their father.

As I stood in the convenience store parking lot, I realized the only tangible thing I had in the entire world was an unopened pack of sugar-free bubblegum.

Later that night, I called Jim and asked him if I could please come back to work. Ten hours later, I was moving bags of concrete and falling deeper and deeper into despair.

16

TIME TO GO HOME

I WAS BROKEN thinking about Taire in that classroom every day. I prayed to God for Him to release her. My heart ached to think of her singing those songs about the devil.

¡Al combate, corred, bayameses!
Que la patria os contempla orgullosa;
No temáis una muerte gloriosa,
Que morir por la patria es vivir.

Run to combat, Bayameses!
Your homeland proudly looks upon you;
Do not fear a glorious death,
For to die for the homeland is to live.

Several weeks passed before Taire and I spoke again. She seemed a bit more normal than she had been recently. There was confidence in her voice—a strength that she was finding in her independence from me. She seemed almost comfortable.

When you are left alone to fend for yourself and for the sake of others, reality becomes whatever your mind tells it to be. Monotony becomes a comfort. The big things are taken care of—food, shelter, work, children.

It was the little things that allowed sadness to creep in almost unnoticed, like late afternoon shadows making their way toward total darkness.

"Things are good," she said. "We're fine."

"Tell me about the kids, Taire. Tell me about you. I miss you so."

She then recounted the following story, and the emotional walls she had been building all this time began to fall apart.

"The other day, a cockroach scurried across the floor and into the kitchen where I was standing. Yusnay screamed and ran to the other room while Orlando and I searched for it under chairs, in cabinets, and on the counter near the sink. The bug was nowhere to be found, so I shrugged and said, 'Oh, well, niño. We tried.' Orlando looked at me, stone-faced, and then lowered his brow: '*Papá hubiera podido.*' Dad could have done it. Then he slowly left the room."

She started to cry.

"But things are good, Yosely. Really, we're fine."

*   *   *

NOVEMBER 2003

The days turned into weeks and the weeks into months. I called the gas station every day, but only spoke to Taire a few times. My promises were falling on deaf ears, and I was beginning to believe that everything I had gained by coming to America was resulting in the ultimate loss of the only things I truly cared about.

I needed another plan.

Alberto called me on a Tuesday. I remember the day because Jim always took our crew to lunch on Tuesdays. Other days, we were responsible for bringing our own food to work, but Jim used to smile and say, "Tuesdays are for tacos."

We were standing in line at Taco Bell when my phone rang:

"Yosely, we found another way." Alberto's voice was low, almost a whisper. "You have to get back to Miami," he said. "Rúben has a plan for Taire. This plan will work."

"Tell me!" I yelled, still standing in the middle of the restaurant. "Alberto, talk to me. What plan?"

Jim put his hand on my shoulder and motioned for me to follow him out of the restaurant, where he stood with me for more than fifteen minutes listening to Alberto describe what was about to happen before he hung up.

"Yosely, what is it? Is it your family?" Jim looked at me and knew that I was about to weep.

"Oh, Jim. I don't know if I can do this." My voice trembled and my heart raced. I felt light-headed as I told him of Rúben's new plan to get my family out of Cuba. It was going to be expensive—very expensive—and I would have to do something I had sworn I never would.

"Are you going to do it?" Jim asked, trying to position himself in my line of sight. I couldn't look up from the ground. I could hardly breathe trying to do the math and calculate the potential cost—both literal and figurative—in my head.

"Yosely, what are you going to do?" Jim persisted.

Then, as if waking from a dream, I rubbed my eyes and breathed in as deeply as I could. I raised my head and looked at Jim, tightened my jaw, and exhaled, "I am going to work. And in three months, I am going to save my family."

The other workers on the crew had finished eating and slowly came out of Taco Bell into the parking lot where Jim and I were standing. Jim didn't say a word. He just kept staring at me, eyes glistening, unable to process what was about to happen. But I was fully aware, and for the first time since pushing our tiny boat away from the rocks at Playa Nazabal, I had a definable goal.

I averaged about eighty dollars per day working for Jim. Some days, it was more, depending on the size of our crew and the difficulty of the jobs that needed to be completed. For instance, cleaning job sites was considered moderate work and yielded minimum payment. Concrete work and hauling materials meant more labor and usually paid between ten and twenty more dollars per day. In reality, Jim used a fairly random method of determining wages, but he almost always made it very much worth our while to wait for his truck in the mornings, rather than jumping in with a different crew that departed earlier from the hardware store.

In addition to crew work, I was continuing small carpentry projects at Linda's art studio and at the Houstons' home. Most weeks, I could make between $600 and $800, but I was going to need a lot more than that if I was going to take Rúben up on his offer.

Several days passed. I hardly ate, slept, or stopped working to even take a sip of water. Jim approached me several times throughout each day imploring me to rest, to stop and talk with him, to at least hydrate between hauls. But work equaled money, and I simply could not afford to stop.

At night, when I was alone, terrible thoughts would run through my head:

I can steal the money. The clerk at the gas station on the corner likes me. I can get close to her and simply take what I need. Or my sister. Yuny keeps things that are important to her under her mattress. She probably has thousands of dollars hidden just on the other side of this wall. Or Jim! He has plenty of money. Probably more than he can count. I could take it from him. I could take his truck! It must be worth double or triple what I need!

I had $16,000. I needed another $8,000. Twice that if I was going to keep my promise to Enier: "I'll send for you. All of you."

I closed my eyes and dreamed of my family. Enier was there too. They were smiling, happy, and waving to me over the railing of a huge ship. I was in a small boat—my boat—alone. The harder I paddled, the farther away they got, still smiling and waving, but moving faster and farther away. I paddled as fast as my arms would let me until finally the ship disappeared beyond the curved horizon. Gone.

I woke drenched in sweat, screaming, with tears streaming down my face. With a stuttered exhale I said aloud, "*Para mi familia.*" For my family.

My mind was made up. I was going to steal Jim's truck, drive it to Miami, sell it, and give Rúben his money. Somehow, some way, I would pay Jim back. But that was a different problem altogether. Right now, my family needed me.

A few hours later, I met the truck as always at the hardware store. Jim invited me to sit in the cab with him, but I refused. I sat in the bed of the truck with the others. When we arrived at the job site, Jim motioned for me to come with him, but I pretended not to see him. I unloaded the bags of concrete at breakneck speed, planning my escape. Jim always put his keys under the driver's side floor mat. It wouldn't be difficult. Just a few more bags, and I'd be gone.

I opened the door to the truck and reached under the seat. The keys. As I put them in my pocket, Jim came up behind me and put his hand on my shoulder.

"Yosely! I got you!" I was so startled I could hardly breathe. The look on Jim's face was serious, and I immediately became paranoid. Maybe he knew what I was planning. But how?

"I'm sorry, Jim. I was going to pay you back." *Why did I say that?* The words slipped out before I could think.

Jim's face tightened and he squinted: "Pay me back? For what?"

I couldn't speak.

"Don't worry about it." He waved his hands and guided me away from the truck. "Listen, I've been trying to get your attention all morning. I need to talk with you about something."

I could hardly swallow. I looked at Jim, frightened about what he might say. We walked for what seemed like a mile without speaking. When we were finally out of earshot from the other workers, Jim leaned against a tree and whispered, "Yosely." He lowered his voice even more. "Linda and I have

been talking—praying, really—about you and your family."
I could feel my heart pounding in my chest, like it was trying to escape.

"Mi familia?" I repeated.

"Yeah. Listen, friend. I've never seen anyone work as hard
as you do. I've never seen someone with your focus, determination, and skill. And I know why you do it. It's unreal—the
love you have for your wife and kids. You have taught me a
lot about what's really important, Yosely, and I—we, Linda
and me—we want to help you."

I reached into my pants pocket, wrapped my fingers
around the truck keys, and squeezed them as tightly as I
could.

"I don't understand, Jim. You want to help me do what?"
I asked.

"We're going to give you the money you need," he smiled.
"We want to help bring your family home."

My desperation and panic turned into a relief that I had
never known. The sudden rush of adrenaline made me feel
nauseous, and I collapsed into Jim's arms. With my face
pressed firmly against his chest, I began to weep. Jim awk-
wardly put his arms around me and squeezed—like he was
the father I had needed my entire life and I was the son he
could never have.

"There, there," he said with his voice cracking. "We're
happy to do it."

Trying to regain my composure, I promised over and over
to pay him back. "Every penny, señor. I will pay you back
every cent."

Jim gave me one last squeeze and wiped his eyes. "We'll make sure you have what you need when it's time. But for now, we've got some work to do. Come on, now. We're burning daylight."

As Jim and I made our way up the hill, we saw the rest of the crew, who had stopped and were standing there. I guessed what they were thinking. *I'm sure they're wondering what I did to make Jim pull me away.* Jim yelled, "Vámonos, amigos! We've got a lot to get done before quittin' time!"

I quickly opened the door to the truck, took the keys out of my pocket, and carelessly threw them under the driver's seat. Jim looked at me, confused, and then motioned for me to get to work.

That afternoon, I had the strength of ten men, and I worked harder and faster than I ever had. I don't think my feet even touched the ground. When I got home, I called Alberto to let him know I was coming to Miami.

✳ ✳ ✳

FEBRUARY 2004

When I arrived in Miami three days later, Alberto met me at the bus station. No niceties were exchanged. No smiles or hugs or hellos.

"*¿Tienes el dinero?*" Do you have the money? "Yes," I answered, pulling the blue duffel bag close to my chest.

"*¿Todo?*" he asked, eyebrows raised. All of it?

"Yes, Alberto. I have all of it. I told you . . ."

He cut me off midsentence and leaned closer. "Because

if you do not have all of it, Rúben will not be happy. He has gone out of his way to do this for you. We both have."

"I understand." I followed him to a large black car idling around the corner.

Alberto's coldness made me angry. Had he already forgotten why I brought us to the United States in the first place? Did he not understand all that I had been through to get to this point?

"Eight thousand each," he said, reaching for the bag. "Two adults and two children."

"Two adults and two children?" I asked angrily, pulling the bag from his hands. "Two adults and two children?" I repeated. "This is my family you are talking about. This is Enier! How dare you speak of them as if they are just cargo you can check off a list. Taire. Orlando. Yusnay. Enier . . ."

"Forgive me, amigo. I'm sorry." Alberto walked to the back of the car. "Of course. I'm sorry. But this is my business now. Put the money in the trunk and let me go get your family." Giving my face a slight slap, he opened the trunk of the car and pointed. I slowly removed the strap from across my chest and gently laid the bag in the back. Alberto slammed the trunk closed and raced to get in the car.

"Rúben will be in touch, my friend!" he yelled as he got in the front seat. "Have a safe trip home."

That was it. My entire savings, Jim's gift, and my family's future sped away in a black sedan being driven by an idiot wearing orange shoes. I closed my eyes and breathed deeply. After traveling on the bus for almost twenty-four hours, I had been on the ground in Miami for less than fifteen minutes before purchasing my return ticket to Nashville.

Before I boarded the bus, I called my old friend at the gas station.

"I don't know when it will be," I told Enier, "but you have to be ready. It could be tonight, tomorrow, or next week. All I know is this is it. Tell me you understand."

Enier was very quiet on the other end of the phone. "I understand, Yosely," he finally answered. "So, we'll see you soon, then?"

"Yes, amigo. Very soon. Tell Taire not to be afraid."

"I will," he said, and then added, "Yosely?" He paused for a few seconds. "Do you really think this will work?"

"You can do this, Enier. I'm counting on you, hermano."

"I understand, Yosely," he said again, and then quietly hung up the phone.

* * *

Yuny and Mikel picked me up from the bus station when I got back to Nashville the next night. I must have looked awful. I hadn't showered or slept in more than three days, and I wore my worry like a wilted mask.

"Yosely, are you okay?" Yuny asked as she reached for my hand. "You left without saying goodbye or telling anyone where you were going. Is it Taire? The kids? Who do you keep going to see in Florida? Are you in trouble?" Squeezing my hand harder and harder with each question, she started to cry.

"It's okay, niña. It's almost over." I forced a quick smile and wiped the tear from her cheek. "Everything will be okay. I promise. Everything will be okay," I repeated, trying to convince her and myself that I hadn't just made a devastating mistake in Miami. *Can I really trust Alberto? Is Rúben really going to do as he promised? Will I ever hear from either one of them again? Will I ever see my family?*

As we pulled into Yuny's apartment complex, my phone buzzed.

The text read: "It's time. *Sábado*. 21:00."

Saturday. That's two days. Oh, dear God, be with them.

* * *

MARCH 6, 2004

Early Saturday morning, I called Jim to see if I could come to his house. "Maybe I could work on the studio for Linda?" I suggested. "Or I could try to finish the fencing around the back field. I could take a look at the gutter on the back side of the main house. I noticed that it was loose . . ."

"Take it easy, amigo." Jim's voice was raspy. "It's five fifteen in the morning on a Saturday," emphasizing that last part as if to question my sanity.

I apologized for calling so early but told him I was hoping to work that day. "I'll do anything," I said.

After a long pause, Jim cleared his throat. "Today is the day, isn't it? Is your family leaving today, Yosely?"

"*Sí*," I responded softly, almost afraid to acknowledge what was happening in Havana.

"Yosely! This is great news, buddy! It's finally happening! Aren't you excited?"

I was not excited. I was terrified. "Jim, I need to work today. Please."

"Okay, my friend." He sensed my impending panic. "I'm sure we can find something for you to do, but it's Saturday. Don't you want to take the day off? Maybe you could just come for lunch."

"Thank you, but I would like to do something. I'm on my way." I hung up the phone before he could respond and asked Mikel to drop me off at Jim's. Within an hour, I was replacing broken, cracked, and warped slats on the wooden fence that lined Jim's immense property. He allowed me to drive his truck, filled with tools and wooden posts, to the farthest corner of the field, where I lost myself in the job. For hours, I worked in that field. Alone, except for the thoughts of my family.

The feel of the wood took me back to my father's shed: "This tree—this piece of wood—was intended for this purpose. It was created for you. It grew in the forest for a hundred years for this purpose."

I took comfort in those words. Maybe I was supposed to be there in that field. Maybe Taire and the kids were exactly where they were supposed to be too. For a brief but beautiful few hours, I felt like everything was going to be okay.

17

BIENVENIDO, MÉXICO

ON SUNDAY AFTERNOON, I received a text message from Alberto:

It worked. Rúben will be in touch.

I became light-headed as every emotion rushed throughout my body and escaped as a scream. "It worked! Gracias, Dios! It worked!"

My scream frightened Yuny and Mikel who came running into the room expecting the worst. When Yuny saw my tears and the overwhelming joy on my face, she hugged me. The three of us stood in the living room embracing and crying together.

"Where is she?" Yuny finally asked.

"I don't know," I responded frantically. "I don't know anything!" I started punching numbers into my phone.

"Alberto said that it worked, but I don't know where they are!" I was screaming and crying and laughing and trying to breathe as deeply as I could. The pressure of the last year—of my entire life—had just been lifted. But now I was floating without a tether or any indication of what was about to happen. "It worked." *What had worked, exactly?*

Alberto picked up after the first ring. "Yosely! Not now,"

he said softly. I could tell he was angry. "I told you that Rúben would be in touch. Trust me, okay?"

"Alberto, please!" I begged. "Please just tell me where they are. I need to know where they are!"

"I don't know. There has been a change in plans. That's all I can tell you. Now, please, do not call me again."

With that, the line went dead. The dial tone echoed in my ears, and I stood, frozen, holding the phone like it was a bomb about to explode.

"A change in plans?" I said aloud to no one. "What kind of change?"

* * *

MARCH 8, 2004

Monday came and went, a nightmare in slow motion. Alberto was not answering my calls, and I hadn't heard anything from Rúben. When I didn't show up for work on Monday morning, Jim got worried and came to Yuny's apartment that evening.

I told him about my bizarre conversation with Alberto the day before. Tears filled his eyes. "What are you going to do?"

I had been asking myself the same question for the past thirty hours, and the only thing I could imagine was going to Miami to confront Rúben in person. "I don't know where he lives," I told Jim, "but I do know where I can find him."

Jim offered to go with me to Miami, but I assured him I needed to go by myself. He also offered to buy me a bus ticket, but the thought of sitting on a bus for the next twenty-four hours made me sick to my stomach.

"I need your truck." I looked at Jim, as serious as I had ever been. He nodded and put the keys in my hand.

"Of course."

It is 913 miles from Yuny's apartment to Miami. I made the drive in less than thirteen hours, arriving at the boatyard in Coconut Grove just before lunchtime on Tuesday. I made several attempts to reach Alberto throughout the night, but he never answered, so I went to find Chino.

"*¡Amigo!*" Chino smiled wide, blew smoke, and flicked his cigarette to the side as he approached the truck. "Don't tell me you need another boat! Didn't you already learn your lesson?"

He began laughing and leaned down to greet me at the window. My rage had been building all night. I was exhausted. I was afraid. I was angry. I put the truck in park and quickly reached out to grab a handful of Chino's hair. He shrieked and held his arms straight out to his sides, flailing and screaming, "*¿Qué estás haciendo?*" What are you doing?

I demanded he tell me where to find Alberto as he begged me to let him go. "Where is he?" I pulled even harder.

Chino insisted that he hadn't seen his cousin in over a week, but that he had overheard him talking about Mexico. He said that Alberto was very upset.

He started to cry and pleaded for me to stop pulling his hair. I released my grip and began to apologize, but he ran away before I could explain.

"*¡Estás loco, idiota!*" he screamed, holding up his middle finger, and then disappeared into the shed behind the docks. You're crazy, you idiot!

Mexico? What could possibly be in Mexico? The only other place I could think to look for Alberto and Rúben was the restaurant in Miami. I pulled into a gas station and asked for directions to the Forge. The clerk looked at me like I was crazy. "The Forge? Really?" she asked. "You're going to the Forge looking like that?"

I caught a glimpse of myself in the security monitor behind the counter. I was a complete mess. My shirt was stained with coffee and grease, I was wearing ill-fitting work pants and boots, and I hadn't shaved or even showered in I don't know how long.

I asked, again, for the fastest route to get to the restaurant. She must have seen the darkness behind my eyes because she quickly called out directions. I committed each turn to memory and ran as fast as I could to the parking lot.

When I reached the truck, my heart almost stopped. My phone was ringing.

"Hello?"

"Hello, Yosely. It's Alberto."

"Alberto! Where have you been?"

"I'm sorry, my friend. I can explain."

"Explain what? Where is my family?"

"Chino called. I'm glad you are in Miami."

"Where is Taire?"

"She's safe, Yosely. They all are."

"Where are they?"

"Where are you?

"I'm on my way to your boss's restaurant."

"Perfect. Come to the restaurant. We need to talk."

I could tell my old friend's voice was trembling before he

ended the call. His words kept repeating over and over in my head: *She's safe, Yosely. They all are.* But the next twenty minutes were some of the longest of my life. When I arrived at the Forge, the parking lot was full. *How can people be eating at a time like this?*

Alberto was waiting for me and waved for me to pick him up. He jumped in the truck and told me to drive. "Where are we going, Alberto?" I screamed and demanded he tell me what was happening.

"Yosely, I have been trying to figure out how to tell you . . ." He was breathing hard as if he had been running.

"Tell me what? You said they are okay!"

"Turn here." He pointed to a side street and told me to stop.

"They are okay. At least we think so. Rúben has been in touch with the boat owner, and he says that everyone is fine. Only one person didn't make it, but he was an old man. Taire and the kids are alive."

I started to cry. "Alberto, where are they?"

He stiffened and then exhaled. "Yosely." Pausing again, he looked away and proceeded to tell me that Enier didn't make the journey. "Rúben received a call two days ago. There is no record of Enier getting on the boat."

I swallowed hard, fighting back tears and aching for my friend. "Where is Taire?" I managed to whisper again. "Where?"

Returning his eyes to mine, Alberto very calmly said, "They are being held in Mexico."

18

PROMISES KEPT

ALBERTO TOOK ME to an office complex just outside of Miami, where he said Rúben would have answers to my questions. We entered the building and were greeted by a young American lady with yellow hair, snow-white teeth, and bright red lipstick.

"Hi, there!" She smiled. "How can I help you?"

"Where's Rúben?" I asked, loud enough for anyone who might be in the building to hear as I started looking frantically past the front desk to the vast hallway behind her.

Still smiling, she responded in a high-pitched voice, "Oh, I'm sorry. Mr. Rodriguez is busy right now. May I tell him what this is regarding?"

I stormed past her and began screaming, "Rúben! Come out here! Rúben! Where is my family?"

A door at the end of the hall opened and Rúben appeared, motioning for me to come. "It's okay, Cynthia!" he called out to the young lady. "He's a friend! Yosely, it's good to see you. Come sit with me."

Rúben stepped aside and offered me a seat. "Alberto, wait for us out front, please." Alberto nervously stepped back toward the lobby, and Rúben slowly closed the door.

"Why is my family in Mexico?" I demanded and moved toward Rúben like a boxer ready to strike.

Holding his hands up as if to concede defeat, Rúben told me to have a seat, but I refused.

"They were supposed to be here by now! You promised me—"

"I promised nothing!" Rúben interrupted me and then slowly sat down at his desk. His tone strengthened. "We had an agreement—a business transaction—and I held up my end."

"A business transaction? No! This is my family! This is my life!" I exclaimed. "I gave you everything, and you have given me nothing!"

I wanted to put fear into Rúben. I wanted to threaten him. I wanted to *make* him find my family. But the facade was starting to crumble. I covered my face with my hands and fell to my knees, weeping.

"Please, please, please . . ." I just kept crying over and over. "I'll do anything," I said. "I'll do anything you want."

Suddenly, I felt a hand on my shoulder. When I opened my eyes, Rúben was standing next to me, his eyes red and swollen.

"*Lo sé, amigo,*" he said. I know, friend. "I know you will."

He helped me to my feet and offered me a seat. "You have endured more than I can possibly imagine, Yosely. More than anyone should have to endure. And for what? *Love?*" He walked to the window and stared at nothing for what seemed like minutes.

Making his way back to sit with me, he continued, "You remember that my parents were Cuban?" I nodded and took in a staggered breath. After a long pause, Rúben lowered his gaze to meet my eyes.

"I know the men who took your wife and children. They don't care about family. They don't care about Cuba. They certainly don't care about love." Rúben stood, slowly walked back behind his desk, and pushed a button on his telephone.

"Cynthia, please send in Alberto," he said. "Oh, and call my wife to let her know I won't be home for dinner."

Turning his attention back to me, Rúben lowered his voice and said, "I am going to help you get your family. And *that* . . . is a promise."

* * *

MARCH 12, 2004

Two days passed and we heard nothing from Rúben. Alberto called several times on the first day but then refused to interfere with or alter his boss's plans on the second. "We have to trust him, Yosely. He is a good man."

A good man? Rúben? What does that even mean—to be good?

I was beginning to question whether good existed anywhere at all. Rúben made his money preying on the weaknesses of others. At the very least, he was a human trafficker, and I had more than a few reasons to suspect that he was also a drug dealer. He operated out of fear and used his power to create fear in others. A good man? Was he any better than Fidel?

"He keeps his promises," Alberto continued. "He said that he was going to save your family, so that is what he will do."

"So why hasn't he called? Where is he? Maybe the Mexicans have him too!" I was beginning to panic, and waiting in that apartment was killing me.

Later that afternoon, the phone finally rang.

"Yosely?"

"Taire? Oh, thank God! Taire, are you okay?"

"Yosely, you have to pay. Please give them what they want."

"I am trying, my love. I promise."

"We don't have much time."

"What do you mean? Are you in danger?"

"Please give them what they want. We don't have much time."

"Taire? What's happening? Are the children okay?"

The call lasted less than fifteen seconds, and she was gone again. Taire's voice was panicked and obviously rehearsed, but at least I knew she was alive. I ran over to Alberto, who was asleep on the couch, and slapped him. "I'm leaving!" I announced. "Tell your boss that if he can't save my family, I have to try!"

Alberto tried to talk me out of going, but I had no choice. I could hardly breathe in that apartment. My body ached, exhausted from holding back a million tears. I grabbed the keys to Jim's truck and pushed myself to the parking lot, gasping for air, desperate to get out of there.

My friend called after me, "Yosely! Wait!" I turned and looked at him standing at the balcony railing with tears streaming down his face.

"¡Dios está contigo, amigo!" God is with you, friend.

I stood, looking at him for a moment, surprised but

comforted, if for only a breath. "*Siempre.*" Always. I nodded and then pulled out of the complex, not having a clue where I was going. The only information I had was that Taire and the kids were in Mexico. I didn't know where exactly, but I knew it was at least a full day's drive from Miami to the closest border crossing.

I'd have to drive through the night.

After more than twelve hours of continuous driving, I pulled off at a rest stop near New Orleans, Louisiana. I don't remember falling asleep, but I was startled awake by my phone ringing.

It was a number I had never seen.

19

"ESTA ES AMÉRICA"

I PICKED UP the phone and hesitantly pressed the call button, afraid to speak.

"Hello?" Rúben's familiar voice both comforted and infuriated me. "Yosely? Is that you, amigo?"

"Rúben! *¡Imbécil!* Where have you been?" I lashed out, sitting straight up and slamming my fist against the steering wheel. "I've been driving all night. Where are you? I'm coming to Mexico. Just tell me where you are. Tell me where my family is . . ." My speech was erratic and becoming more and more elevated with each word.

Interrupting calmly, Rúben shushed me, "My friend. My friend. *Tranquilízate, ¿sí?*" Take it easy, okay? "Someone would like to say hello."

After a brief pause, I heard my Taire.

"Hola? Yosely? I don't know what's happening. Yosely, is this really you?"

I was overtaken by tears and kept repeating, "Sí, sí, sí," over and over. Orlando's voice rang out in the background: "Papá!" I could tell that they were in a car.

"Taire, you can trust Rúben," I said. "He is a friend. Just do as he says, okay? Everything is going to be alright."

"He saved us, Yosely. We were being held by some awful men, and he saved us," she said, over and over.

"Let me talk to him, my love. I need to speak with Rúben."

Rúben quickly told me what had happened.

A man he referred to as "Santiago" had been holding Taire and many others for ransom. He thought that if people like me were willing to pay to get their families out of Cuba, they would pay even more to get them into America. Rúben used to do business with Santiago and knew exactly where he was keeping my family.

"How much did you have to pay?" I questioned Rúben over and over. "What did you do? How? Where are you? How did you get them? Can I meet you? How did you know where they were? Rúben, how much do I owe you?"

"Santiago owes me money, Yosely," Rúben said calmly. "A lot of money. It turns out I can be very convincing when money is involved. Your debt is paid in full, and tomorrow, mine will be too. Your family is safe now, my friend." His voice cracked as he told me that he had twenty-three other people who would also be making the trip to the border in Brownsville, Texas.

Twenty-three. Dear God.

"We will all be there tomorrow. All of us." And then he began to cry.

"Tomorrow?" I asked, hoping I had heard him correctly.

"Sí, hermano. Tomorrow, your family will be free."

For the past two years, I had been only half alive. Numb

ESTA ES AMÉRICA"

and barely breathing. Just surviving, not living. Without my family, I felt like a stone sinking farther and farther into the depths. There were times I wanted to give up. Stop trying. Stop rowing. Stop swimming. Stop driving. Stop working. Stop hoping. But in that moment—in a borrowed truck on the outskirts of New Orleans—I was reborn.

Finally, and for the first time in my life, I was fully alive and fully aware of the significance of what tomorrow might bring.

I turned the key, rolled my windows down, and like an infant after his first breath, let out a scream that rushed through me like an ocean surge. It was relief and anxiety, pleasure and pain, happiness and complete terror. It was a scream containing more than five hundred years of struggle, rebellion, and a dream. The once-and-for-all letting go of oppression and desperation. A full embrace of hope, faith, love, and redemption.

* * *

MARCH 14, 2004

I had driven Jim's truck almost three thousand miles since leaving Nashville less than a week before. But my family's story didn't start there. A simple wooden boat had carried me the span of the Florida Straits, but the journey didn't start there, either. I'd spent two years alone, waiting for this day. Working until my fingers bled. Praying to a God who promised to be with me always. Looking for Him to show up, to somehow protect the people I love.

A lifetime of wondering, working, struggling, and

dreaming had finally brought me within reach of my family—free for the first time in our lives. *Is this really happening? Is today the day?*

As I pulled closer and closer to the man-made barrier that separated me from Taire, Orlando, and Yusnay, I wondered if God was watching, if He was really there. I thought about the people in my life who had helped us.

My father, who taught me how to build a boat. "The measurements have to be perfect, Yosely. Otherwise, the boat will not sail in a straight line." The prisoner who somehow found the courage to share his Bible with me. "Hold on to this. It will protect you," he said.

I couldn't have understood it then, but he opened a door that day that allowed hope to become more than a wish. It was an expectation.

I thought about Neo, God rest his soul, and the other passengers on that enfeebled craft. Rafael, Javier, Alberto. None of us would have made it to America's shores without the others. Gratitude overcame me. I thought about Jim and the perfect example of kindness, acceptance, and grace he represented in my life. And Rúben, an unlikely hero who was currently delivering my family to freedom.

Maybe that's what God was trying to say when He promised to always be with me. Maybe He was working through all the people—all the ups and downs throughout my life— to bring me here to this point.

To my family.

Before I hung up the phone with Rúben the night before, he gave me strict instructions for when I reached the border. "Wait for your family on the bridge," he said. "When you arrive at the border, it will look like a circus. There will be hundreds of cars, trucks, buses, and passenger vans crossing in both directions. But don't be afraid," he said. "This will all be over soon."

"Rúben?" I managed to stop him from hanging up.

"*¿Sí, hay algo más?*" Yes, is there something else?

"Why are you doing this?" I asked. "Why are you risking so much for me?"

"Why?" He sounded as if he were about to weep. He took a deep breath. "Love," he finally whispered.

"Yosely, I have never even allowed myself to dream about a love like you have for your family," he said. "When something that pure and powerful exists, you can't turn your back on it, amigo. You do whatever you can to keep it alive. Even I know that." He paused. "We'll see you tomorrow."

* * *

MARCH 15, 2004: 11:00 A.M.

During the short drive from Monterrey, Mexico, to the Texas border, Rúben had Taire call to make sure I knew where they would be. "Rúben says that we should be there by one o'clock. Will you be there?"

"I'm here now, my love," I said through tears. The anticipation of their arrival just two hours later made my chest ache, and the air was pulled mercilessly from my lungs.

"Rúben seems nervous, Yosely," she whispered quietly into the phone.

"Nervous about what? Does he have your papers?"

"Sí. He has everything. Everything is perfect. But he has

been very nervous, looking in his mirrors constantly. I think we are being followed."

"Who would be following you?" I asked. Now *I* was getting nervous. Was it the police? Was it Santiago and the kidnappers?

"Who is following you, Taire? Please answer me!"

The line was quiet.

"I don't know," she finally whispered and then started to cry. "There are vans behind us, Yosely. White vans. Four of them. *Dios nos salve.*" God help us.

Rúben's voice suddenly boomed, "You have to hang up now! Hurry, give me the phone!" I heard Yusnay crying in the background and Taire yelling, "What's happening?"

And then . . . silence.

I was in anguish for about thirty minutes, maybe longer. I didn't know what to do, where to go, who to call, or how to get in touch with Taire. I was frozen with fear. I couldn't help but imagine what was happening with my family.

Have they been arrested?

Were they run off the road?

Did Santiago and his men catch up to them?

I tried calling over and over again. I must have dialed a hundred times, to no avail. I left Jim's truck in a parking lot a few meters from the border control building and began running toward the crowd that had been gathering at the US side of the border over the last several hours. Ten, twenty, thirty, a hundred people pushed together, many holding signs or waving American flags—each one smiling or crying; all waiting, hoping, and praying to welcome someone they loved.

I became one of them, all of us mumbling desperate prayers, straining our necks and standing on the tips of our toes in hopes that we might get a quicker glimpse of our loved ones. For me, it had been almost twenty-six months. A lifetime. For others, it had been even longer.

Would our great nightmare end at this gate?

Suddenly I saw four white vans—just as Taire had described. They slowly approached the gate. Four sliding doors opened simultaneously and people poured out, one after another: women and children, over and over. There were so many.

So, so many.

I was frozen, watching these terrified souls scamper out of the vans and approach the guards at the gate. Some were running. Others approached timidly, as if tiptoeing toward a lion's cage. I listened as they sheepishly shared their papers and spoke the words they had been rehearsing for the past two days:

"We escaped Cuba. We are seeking asylum in the United States. We escaped Cuba. We are seeking asylum in the United States."

One after another they stood, shaking, begging for their freedom.

Over the heads of the masses, I saw a woman with blonde hair, wearing a blue dress, back out of the passenger side of a large green car. She leaned across the front seat and gave the driver a kiss.

Out of the back door, a small boy jumped to the concrete and excitedly grabbed the woman's right hand. In her other arm she was holding a baby, a little girl who was fast asleep.

They made their way through the line of people waiting to speak with the armed guards standing shoulder to shoulder at the crossing to a bridge.

"*¿Qué esta pasando, Mama?*" What's going on? The little boy called up to his mother, still holding her hand. "*¿Estamos en los Estados Unidos?*" he stuttered. Are we in the United States?

An American police officer overheard the question and knelt to meet the little boy's eyes. "*Sí, pequeño.*" Yes, little one. "*Esta es América.*" This is America.

Rising to stand, the officer looked at the woman and smiled. Pointing ahead of them to where I stood with a small group of other anxious and hopeful people, he said, "We've been waiting for you."

Taire's eyes met mine with confusion.

"Yosely?" I saw her mouth move, but she didn't make a sound. Then again, "Yosely!" She screamed, and looked to the officer as if to ask, "Can I?"

Suddenly, Orlando saw me and ran—past the officers, under the security gate—and landed heavily in my arms.

"Papá! Papá! Papá!" he cried over and over, squeezing my neck and burying his head beneath my chin. When I opened my eyes, Taire was in front of me, holding Yusnay, cheeks wet with tears, and smiling. Gently reaching for her hand, I stood and kissed my wife for the first time in 766 days.

"*Te ves cansado,*" she whispered. You look tired.

I held her close, then gathered my entire family in my arms. I still haven't let go.

A WORD FROM
YOSELY & TAIRE

WE HOPE OUR STORY offers readers a glimpse of what is happening each and every day in Cuba. Tens of thousands of people risk their lives each year in an attempt to be freed from communism and provide a better life for themselves and their families.

Thousands are either apprehended and placed in jail or they die trying to navigate the Florida Straits.

The fact that our people have been risking their lives and would rather risk death at sea than continue existing in their homeland is a heartbreaking testimony that this is an ongoing problem—one that will surely continue until communism is defeated and Cuba becomes a free country.

Unfortunately, many Americans lose sight of the great blessing we share living in a free country.

We live in a place where freedom includes the opportunity for prosperity and success for all. A country where "all men are created equal" with the right to "Life, Liberty and the pursuit of Happiness." Are we able to truly enjoy our God-given freedoms knowing what is happening just ninety miles from our shores?

We want to somehow help humanize the generations

of people who have endured the very same things you have read about in the pages of this book—over and over again. We hope that we can help show the true value of these lives and the very real potential that each one has to experience freedom.

Q & A WITH
YOSELY & TAIRE

YOSELY, WHEN YOU WERE PLANNING TO LEAVE CUBA, HOW DID YOU PICTURE AMERICA? WHAT DID YOU HOPE IT WOULD BE LIKE?

Y: I didn't know. I just needed a change. I would see people come back to Cuba after leaving for the United States, and they just looked different. They looked happy and healthy. I knew I needed to find out what that life could mean for my family.

WERE YOU SCARED WHEN YOU WERE BUILDING THE BOAT? AS YOU WORKED ALONE IN THE DARK, WHAT WERE YOU THINKING ABOUT?

Y: I was very nervous, but it was worth it. It was not safe. It was very dangerous. But *not* building the boat was scarier to me. I thought about my family on those nights, about possibly losing them forever. But if there was even a small chance for me to provide a better life for them outside of Cuba, I was willing to risk everything. I was even willing to die because death is better than living there. There is no chance for a happy life there.

TAIRE, DID YOU KNOW THAT YOSELY WAS BUILDING A BOAT? DID YOU KNOW THAT HE WAS DESPERATE TO LEAVE?

T: I knew he wanted to leave, and I knew *why* he wanted to escape— for us—but I was more focused on my children. I was more focused on surviving in Cuba. It's difficult for people to understand the situation people were in and are still experiencing there. Yosely had no choice. He was being pursued every day by the police. He couldn't work. He couldn't sell his furniture. The children were starving. And there was literally nothing he could do about it. He tried so hard to protect us every day, but the government had his arms and legs tied behind his back. He had to go. He had to at least try.

WHAT WAS MISSING FROM YOUR LIFE IN CUBA? WHAT DID YOU HOPE FOR?

T: Hope is a very difficult thing in Cuba. It's not that hope does not exist; we just don't know how to find it. We don't even know what to look for. Every time you try to do something—to take initiative and try something different or new—every time you try to fly, they come and clip your wings.

You wake up every day to the same day. There is no thought that "tomorrow will be better; tomorrow will be happy; tomorrow we will not be hungry or sad or scared." Every day is another day to endure.

Can you imagine the desperation it takes for a human being to get in a boat and row into the darkness just for the chance of a different day?

TAIRE, HOW WERE YOU ABLE TO RECONCILE THE FACT THAT YOSELY LEFT YOU AND THE CHILDREN?

T: There were several stages of fear and nervousness those first few days. I was very scared for his safety. But the second I knew he was safe, I finally cried. I was so happy for him, but I was also relieved because I *knew* Yosely was going to find a way to bring us to freedom. I never doubted that. I thought, *My children will not have to grow up the way I did; they won't have to live in poverty; they will not have to live in fear; they will never be tortured and lied to; they will have a future to be excited about.*

However, I didn't think it would take as long as it did. Two or three months, maybe. Not more than two years.

IF YOU HAD KNOWN IT WOULD TAKE THAT LONG, WOULD YOU HAVE FELT DIFFERENTLY ABOUT YOSELY BEING IN THE UNITED STATES WITHOUT YOU? AND WHAT ABOUT YOU, YOSELY?

T: Yosely was very sad without us, but I had to make him promise to stay in the United States and keep working to bring us home. I would tell him, "Send me a piece of wood and we will float to you. We will do whatever you tell us to do. Just do not lose your freedom."

Y: After just six months, I wanted to return to Cuba. I was willing to give up my freedom just to see my family. I missed them more than I ever thought possible. There were days when I thought I would have been better off if I had died on that boat. I was completely broken without them.

HOW DID PEOPLE IN CUBA REACT TO YOSELY LEAVING?

T: Some people were proud of him. Some people were happy. But there are a lot of brainwashed people there who thought he was a traitor and they turned their backs on us as well. But that is not their fault. They don't have a choice. From the moment Cuban children are old enough to understand, they are taught that Fidel is God, that the United States is evil, and that we are so lucky because no other country has as much as we do. And you know what? We believe it.

WHAT HAPPENED TO ENIER?

Y: Enier made it to America! He is free! He now lives in Miami and is still my closest friend. A few years ago, Enier became a US citizen, and he is now married and has three children. I owe Enier everything. I owe him my life because he helped save my family. I still talk to him often. Every year on my birthday, he is the first person to call.

T: I love that man, and I thank God for him every day for what he did for our family. He was sent from God to Yosely, and Yosely sent him to protect our family.

WHAT HAPPENED TO THE OTHER PASSENGERS IN YOUR BOAT?

Y: I know that they are in Florida, but we have all moved on and created separate lives. I think of them often and wish my old friends well, but we are not in touch.

WHAT WERE YOUR FIRST THOUGHTS WHEN YOU SAW EACH OTHER FOR THE FIRST TIME AFTER YOU CROSSED THE BORDER AND WERE SAFE?

T: I was scared. I was very nervous. I didn't know what to expect. I was happy to see Yosely and hugged him as tightly as I could, but I was mostly scared for the first few months after coming here. I was scared we were going to be sent back.

Y: The first word I said was "Taire! Taire!" The first words she said to me were, "You look tired." Later, she told me I had gotten fat. That's a true story. Those were her first thoughts when she saw me!

HOW OFTEN DO YOU GO BACK TO VISIT YOUR FRIENDS AND FAMILY IN CUBA?

T: There used to be restrictions—maybe three times a year—but there is no restriction today. We can go any time we want, but I would not return if it weren't for my family there. My mother and father and sister and nephews are there, and I need to see them. If they were not there, I would not go back to that place.

DO YOU MISS ANYTHING ABOUT CUBA?

T: I miss my language. I miss hearing the beautiful language that I grew up speaking. I speak English now, but it is not my language.

Y: I miss the culture of the people. I miss the community. I miss my friends. But I do not miss that country. Cuba is a hell on earth.

IF YOU HAD NOT ESCAPED CUBA TO COME TO THE UNITED STATES, WHAT DO YOU THINK YOUR LIVES WOULD BE LIKE TODAY?

Y: We talk about this a lot. Especially after we go back to see family. Basically, I think I would probably be in prison or dead. I do not think I could have survived the last eighteen years there.

T: I cannot imagine what life would be like for me, but I have nightmares about what it would be like for our kids. Yosely is right. He would probably be in prison. Orlando would probably be there as well. I don't know. Maybe he would be an alcoholic. Yusnay would most definitely have become pregnant at a very early age.

Y: We would be destroyed.

ARE YOU WHOLE NOW?

Y: There will always be a broken part of me. Cuba took a lot of my life and a lot of my heart. But I became whole when my family met me at the border. We have been whole since we stepped into this country together.

HOW HAS CUBA CHANGED SINCE YOU ESCAPED?

Y: Cuba has changed a lot since we escaped, but not in a good way. It has gotten much worse. Every time we go back to visit, it seems much worse.

T: The persecution is worse. The police seem to be getting angrier and angrier with citizens—for no reason. We see people being beaten and pushed down in the streets. We see hungry people desperate for food. We endured many of the same things when we lived there, but today it seems to be a much sadder place.

MANY AMERICANS THINK OF HAVANA AS A ROMANTIC CITY AND A WONDERFUL PLACE TO VISIT. CAN YOU SPEAK TO THE REALITY OF LIFE IN THAT CITY?

T: Havana is desperate. It is broken just like the rest of the Island. It is the capital, so there is more opportunity there, but the difference is like having five eggs to eat every week as opposed to two throughout the rest of the country. And the hotels and restaurants in Havana are for tourists, not Cubans. No Cuban citizen can afford to stay at those places. A one-night stay would cost what a Cuban makes in three years.

YOU'VE BEEN IN THE UNITED STATES FOR ALMOST TWO DECADES. IS IT EASY TO FORGET THE LIVES YOU ENDURED BEFORE ESCAPING?

T: I cannot forget, but I fear sometimes taking for granted all that we have now. We have a lot. The one thing I cannot bear is throwing away food. I break down and cry every time a plate of food is thrown away because there are entire families who could eat for a whole day on that generous serving.

Y: I feel like I want to forget, but maybe God reminds me every now and then, so I do not get too comfortable. I don't know. It breaks my heart to want to forget, but I do. I wish I had never lived there.

MARTIN LUTHER KING JR. SAID, "INJUSTICE ANYWHERE IS A THREAT TO JUSTICE EVERYWHERE." DO YOU BELIEVE THAT? KNOWING WHAT IS HAPPENING IN YOUR HOME COUNTRY—JUST NINETY MILES AWAY FROM HERE—ARE YOU ABLE TO BE TRULY HAPPY HERE?

Y: That is a very tough question. I am very happy here because we are blessed with many people and opportunities that help provide for our family and for others. But knowing that people are suffering the way we used to suffer is very difficult.

T: I think that quote is true. Maybe I am not truly happy here, but I am very, very grateful, and I try to never take a single minute of any day for granted.

HOW HAS YOUR FAITH CHANGED SINCE COMING TO THE UNITED STATES?

T: My faith is stronger here because it is out in the open. I never could freely pray. I never felt free to even admit believing in God.

Y: Twenty years ago, praying before a meal could get you sent to prison. People do not understand the fact that faith is not something that exists in Cuba. Being in the United States, we are able to grow in our faith by seeing others worship and practice their religion.

T: We know that God is with us. We are His, and He loves us. He has protected us and provided for us all along the way.

DO YOU STILL KEEP IN TOUCH WITH JIM HOUSTON?

Y: I talk to him a lot. He is still very much a part of our lives.

T: He is one of the kindest humans I have ever met. He helped us more than we could ever repay in a thousand lifetimes.

WHAT WERE THOSE FIRST FEW WEEKS LIKE TOGETHER IN NASHVILLE?

Y: I went to work the very next day. I was afraid not to work. I wanted to make money so we could stay in America and buy a place to live and start our new life. Jim Houston paid our rent and utilities for several months. He even gave us a new television.

T: I watched television nonstop. I was scared to leave our apartment, so I watched American soap operas so I could learn English. And it worked! I picked up the language very quickly.

WHAT ARE YOU DOING NOW?

Y: I have my own carpentry business in Nashville. I can build just about anything and have a lot of very generous clients who hire me to remodel kitchens, build shelves, stairs, bookcases . . . anything. I am very blessed to have consistent work.

T: I am an ESL teacher for school-aged children in Nashville. It is such a blessing to be able to share my experience with them and help them the way so many people have helped me.

WHY IS IT IMPORTANT FOR PEOPLE TO READ AND UNDERSTAND THIS STORY?

Y: I want people to become educated and encouraged by the stories I wish I could forget. It's important to be aware of the things that are happening so close to America. People need to pray for Cuba and help make the United States a more welcoming place for those who are seeking a better life.

T: I think it is important for people to know the story of a man who loves his family so much, he was willing to die for them. And a family who loves that man so much that they were willing to wait for him to find a way to reunite them.

ACKNOWLEDGMENTS

BILLY IVEY

Thank you, all-knowing, all-seeing, all-powerful God—for loving us in spite of us; for being in control even when we fail to see your hand at work. Even when the storms come. Or the words run out.

Thank you, Yosely and Taire. You are my heroes.

Thank you, Chet and Mary Virginia. Your patience, grace, and trust are undeserved and more appreciated than you will ever know. Thank you, Bethany. My heart. Thank you, Anna Beth, for your encouragement. Ben, for your excitement. Merrie Cannon, for your wonder. Abe, for your interest. Quinn, for your questions. You all have made this book better because you are all so perfectly . . . you.

Thank you, Corinne and Brock Kidd, for your places of beauty, escape, and rest.

Thank you, Jon Acuff, for your inspiration and wisdom.

Thanks to Lisa Jackson at Alive Literary, who fell in love with this story and championed this project from the very start. Thanks to Jon Farrar, Bonne Steffen, and the entire team at Tyndale House.

Special thanks to Eric Chapman, Chip Burns, Terri Cox, Michael Ford, Matt Lane Harris, and so many more who helped make this labor of love a reality.

Thanks to the Avett Brothers, Dawes, Band of Horses, David Wilcox, Bob Schneider, and 172 hours and 18 minutes of "Cuban Music" on Spotify for serving as my soundtrack to this story.

And finally, thanks to the people of Cuba—for your strength, beauty, perseverance, resilience, and great love.

Estoy asombrado por todos ustedes.

ABOUT THE AUTHORS

YOSELY PEREIRA has lived in the United States since 2002. Yosely works as a master carpenter, designing and constructing special projects from his workshop in Nashville. His wife, Taire, serves students and parents as a parents' outreach translator and ESL teacher with Metro Nashville Public Schools. Their immediate family lives and works in the greater Nashville region. The couple currently resides in Franklin, Tennessee.

BILLY IVEY lives in Birmingham, Alabama, and has been an advertising writer and branding professional for more than twenty years. Throughout his career, he has partnered with local, regional, and national brands like Chick-fil-A, Home Depot, Major League Baseball, and hundreds more. Billy earned his BA in English literature from Samford University. He and his wife, Bethany, have five children and spend most of their time at baseball, football, wrestling, tennis, dance, cheerleading, show choir, and lacrosse practices.